from zero to hero

Your Journey to Becoming a Data Scientist

william webb

contents

introduction: the world of data science

defining data science

HAVE you ever wondered why your favorite online retailer seems to understand your shopping habits better than you do? Or why your music streaming app never fails to suggest songs that fit your mood perfectly? The invisible puppeteer orchestrating these seemingly magical events is none other than data science.

Data science, in its simplest form, is a multi-disciplinary field that uses scientific methods, processes, algorithms, and systems to extract knowledge and insights from structured and unstructured data. It is the secret recipe that businesses, governments, and organizations use to make sense of the vast amounts of data generated in our digital world.

Let's break it down further. The term "data science" is made up of two distinct words: "data" and "science". Data refers to the facts and statistics collected together for reference or analysis, while science refers to the systematic study of the structure and behavior of the physical and natural world through observation and experiment. When combined, we get a field that is dedicated to the systematic analysis, interpretation, and understanding of data.

It's quite easy to think of data science as a fancy term for statistics. After all, isn't it about analyzing data? Yes, but that's just scratching the surface. While statistics indeed form the backbone of data science, the field is much more diverse and complex.

Data science encompasses a variety of skills and disciplines, including but not limited to mathematics, statistics, computer science, data visualization, machine learning, and domain-specific knowledge. To put it simply, data science isn't just about analyzing data - it's about understanding it, extracting valuable insights from it, and using those insights to make informed decisions or predictions.

Imagine you're the captain of a ship navigating uncharted waters. The raw data is the endless ocean around you, difficult to comprehend in its entirety. As a data scientist, your role is to interpret the ocean currents, decipher the weather patterns, predict the tides, and navigate your ship to its destination. This voyage requires not just statistical tools, but also programming skills, visual aids, and domain knowledge.

Data science is an iterative process. It starts with defining a question or problem, collecting and cleaning the data, exploring and analyzing the data, modeling and interpreting the results, and finally, communicating the findings in an understandable manner. Each of these stages is a critical part of the data science life cycle, requiring a unique set of skills and tools.

Moreover, data science is not restricted to one industry or field. Whether it's finance, healthcare, retail, or even sports, data science has a role to play. It powers recommendation engines on e-commerce sites, helps in predicting disease outbreaks in healthcare, optimizes logistics in manufacturing, and even aids in player selection in sports.

In the era of big data, the ability to extract valuable insights from data is a powerful tool. We generate an astronomical amount of data every day. If harnessed properly, this data can provide invaluable insights, helping businesses improve their products, governments enhance their services, and individuals make better decisions. This transformative potential is what makes data science an exciting and rapidly growing field.

Data science is often referred to as the "sexiest job of the 21st century", and for a good reason. It offers the promise of fascinating work, attractive salaries, and the chance to make a real impact. But it's not just about the glamour. It's about curiosity, creativity, and a passion for problem-solving.

With that said, our voyage into the world of data science is just beginning. There is much more to explore, learn, and understand. As we delve deeper into the field, you'll get a chance to familiarize yourself with the tools, techniques, and practices that data scientists use daily.

We have a thrilling journey ahead of us, filled with discoveries and insights. Hold on tight, because this ride, much like the field of data science itself, promises to be a remarkable one. Remember, every question you answer will lead to new questions, every problem you solve will reveal new challenges, and that's the real beauty of data science.

the importance and impact of data science

Data science, in the simplest terms, is like a modern-day compass guiding us through the vast sea of information available at our fingertips. In the present day, every click, swipe, like, or share we make leaves behind a digital footprint that collectively forms an astronomical amount of data. Data science enables us to tap into this ocean of data to extract useful insights that can help individuals, organizations, and governments make informed decisions.

The importance of data science stems from its unique ability to discover patterns and correlations hidden within this data. By doing so, it allows us to predict future trends, behaviors, and outcomes with increasing accuracy. This predictive power holds immense potential and is one of the reasons why data science is such a transformative force in today's world.

Let's bring this to life with some real-world examples. Imagine you are browsing your favorite online shopping platform. As you scroll, you find that the recommendations are eerily in line with your interests. This is not magic, but rather the power of data science. Retail giants use data science to analyze your browsing and purchasing history, along with that of millions of other users, to provide personalized recommendations that boost sales and customer satisfaction.

Or consider healthcare, an industry where data science has become indispensable. It aids in predicting disease outbreaks, personalizing medical treatments, optimizing hospital operations, and even deciphering the human genome. In essence, data science has the potential to revolutionize healthcare, transforming it from a one-size-fits-all approach to personalized and preventive care.

Data science also plays a pivotal role in social media platforms. It powers the algorithms that decide which posts appear on your feed, analyzes trends to understand what's popular, and even identifies fake news or harmful content. It can also be used to study social behavior and trends on a large scale, providing insights that were previously impossible to obtain.

And these are just a few instances of how data science impacts our lives. It extends to virtually every industry you can think of – from optimizing delivery routes in logistics to predicting climate patterns in environmental science, and from enhancing player performance in sports to combating fraud in finance.

But it's not just industries and businesses that benefit from data science. It also impacts governments and policy-making. Data science can help governments optimize public services, make informed policy decisions, and predict and respond to crises. For instance, during the COVID-19 pandemic, data science played a crucial role in tracking the spread of the virus, predicting hospital needs, and guiding public health decisions.

At its core, data science is a tool – a powerful tool, but a tool nonetheless. It's a means to an end, and that end is to make better, more informed decisions.

Whether it's a business deciding which product to launch, a doctor deciding which treatment to administer, or a government deciding how to allocate resources, data science can help illuminate the path forward.

However, with great power comes great responsibility. As we harness the power of data science, it's critical to use it ethically and responsibly. We must ensure that data privacy and security are maintained, that biases in data and algorithms are identified and mitigated, and that the benefits of data science are accessible to all.

As we continue our journey in the realm of data science, it's important to remember the scale and scope of its impact. This knowledge will give us a better understanding of why the skills and techniques we're about to delve into are so important.

career opportunities in data science

By now, we have a good understanding of what data science is and why it matters. Now, let's shift our focus to something a bit more personal: you. More specifically, let's discuss how data science can shape your career path.

The rise of big data has brought about an explosion of roles in data science. Whether you're a seasoned professional considering a career pivot or a novice teeming with curiosity and eagerness to learn, the field of data science has a place for you. It's a realm brimming with opportunities for those who have the skills and the desire to turn data into meaningful insights.

Let's begin with the most recognized role: the Data Scientist. These are the Sherlock Holmes' of the data world, using their diverse skills in programming, statistics, and domain knowledge to derive insights from data. They formulate questions, design and carry out experiments, and interpret the results to inform decision-making. However, contrary to popular belief, being a data scientist isn't the only way to build a career in this field.

Consider the role of the Data Analyst. They play a crucial part in the data science lifecycle. Their main job is to sift through data and provide reports and visualizations to explain what insights the data is hiding. If you're someone who enjoys finding patterns and telling stories with data, a data analyst role might be the perfect fit.

Then we have the Machine Learning Engineer. They design and build machine learning systems, conduct tests, and implement machine learning algorithms. This role often requires a deeper understanding of computer science and programming. If you're fascinated by AI and how machines can learn from data, this might be the career path for you.

A Data Engineer, on the other hand, handles the design, construction, and maintenance of large-scale processing systems and databases. They ensure data is clean, reliable, and readily available for data scientists and analysts. If you're interested in the architectural side of data handling, you might find data engineering particularly engaging.

On a slightly different note, there's a role for those who are passionate about the intersection of data science and business: the Data Strategist. These individuals understand data from a business perspective, and their main job is to determine how to use data strategically to achieve business goals.

The roles mentioned above are just the tip of the iceberg. The field of data science continues to evolve, leading to a proliferation of specialized roles like the AI Specialist, NLP Scientist, or Business Intelligence Developer, each offering unique challenges and opportunities.

However, don't be too quick to box yourself into one specific title. The fluidity and multidisciplinary nature of data science mean that there is a lot of overlap between these roles. As you grow in your data science journey, you might find yourself wearing multiple hats or transitioning between different roles based on your interests and the needs of your projects.

Moreover, remember that data science is not confined to a specific industry. From tech and finance to healthcare, sports, and even arts and humanities, data science skills are in high demand. The world is your oyster, and data science can be the compass that guides your career in exciting directions.

This diversity of career paths is what makes data science an appealing field for many. It provides an opportunity to constantly learn and evolve, to take on new challenges, and to make a real impact. But remember, a rewarding career in data science doesn't come from the title you hold but the problems you solve, the questions you answer, and the value you bring.

As we prepare to embark on this next stage of our journey, bear in mind that the road to mastering data science is not always straightforward. It demands patience, persistence, and a whole lot of curiosity. But fret not, for the journey itself promises to be as rewarding as the destination. After all, the essence of data science lies in unraveling the unknown, one dataset at a time. Let's gear up and get ready to ride the data wave!

1 /
mathematics for
data science

overview of essential mathematics

AS WE NAVIGATE our path through the captivating realm of data science, it's time we delve into the foundational concepts that underpin much of the work in this field. Yes, you've guessed it - it's time to talk about mathematics.

Now, before the word 'mathematics' sends chills down your spine or evokes flashbacks of your high school algebra class, take a deep breath. Yes, math is a vital part of data science, but it's not about mindlessly crunching numbers or solving abstract equations. It's about understanding patterns, making predictions, and using logical reasoning to make informed decisions - all things that are at the heart of data science.

First on our list is Statistics, a branch of mathematics that's like the beating heart of data science. Statistics provides the tools to collect, analyze, interpret, present, and organize data. As a data science enthusiast, you'll encounter concepts like mean, median, mode, variance, standard deviation, correlation, regression, and hypothesis testing. Grasping these statistical measures will help you understand your data better, uncover insights, and make predictions.

Next up, we have Probability. While statistics help us analyze and understand past data, probability helps us predict what could happen in the future. It's the mathematics of uncertainty, allowing us to make sense of random events and phenomena. Probability theories like Bayes' Theorem often form the bedrock of machine learning algorithms, making it a critical part of your data science toolkit.

Linear Algebra is another essential branch of mathematics for data scientists. While it might sound intimidating, it's simply the study of vectors and certain rules to manipulate them. In data science, we often deal with high-dimensional data - think about a spreadsheet with hundreds of columns. Each of these data points can be considered a vector in a high-dimensional space. Linear algebra helps us manipulate and understand these high-dimensional spaces.

Finally, let's talk about Calculus. This branch of mathematics deals with rates of change and quantities that accumulate. It's instrumental for optimizing machine learning algorithms and understanding how they work. While you won't be solving complicated calculus problems on a daily basis as a data scientist, having a foundational understanding of concepts like derivatives and integrals can be beneficial.

Before we move forward, it's essential to note that you don't need to be a mathematician to become a data scientist. However, having a good grasp of these mathematical foundations will make your data science journey smoother and more rewarding. It's not about memorizing formulas or techniques, but about understanding the underlying logic and reasoning that drives them.

. . .

In the coming Sections, we'll be delving deeper into these mathematical concepts, demystifying them, and showing how they apply in the world of data science. Remember, the goal is not to intimidate you, but to empower you with the tools to navigate the data landscape confidently.

linear algebra

Linear Algebra, at first glance, may seem intimidating. Yet, it's an incredibly vital field in mathematics that allows us to handle multidimensional data efficiently. Fear not, for we're here to unravel its mysteries together, one vector at a time.

Let's start with the basics: vectors and matrices. In the simplest terms, a vector is a list of numbers, and a matrix is a grid of numbers. The numbers in a vector or matrix could represent anything: the characteristics of a customer, pixels in an image, sales over time, and so on. When you hear about 'multidimensional' data in data science, it's often referring to data represented as vectors or matrices.

. . .

Next, we have vector operations, including vector addition and scalar multiplication. These are fundamental operations in linear algebra that allow us to manipulate and combine vectors in different ways. For example, if we represent customers as vectors, vector addition could be a way to find an 'average' customer.

Linear combinations and spans are two more essential concepts. A linear combination is a combination of vectors with specific weights or coefficients. The 'span' of a set of vectors is the set of all possible linear combinations. In practical terms, this helps us understand how different data points relate to each other and how we can create or predict new data points.

Another critical operation in linear algebra is the dot product. The dot product of two vectors is a single number that can tell us about the vectors' similarity. This operation forms the basis of many machine learning algorithms, including support vector machines and neural networks.

Then, there's the concept of a matrix, and operations like matrix multiplication, transpose, and inversion.

Matrices can represent transformations of data. For example, rotating an image, reducing the dimensions of data, or translating a dataset are all achieved through matrix operations.

A particularly important concept is eigenvectors and eigenvalues. These allow us to understand the 'essence' of a matrix transformation. They're critical in many advanced data science techniques, including principal component analysis (PCA), which is used for dimensionality reduction.

Now, if all this sounds a little abstract, that's because it is! But fear not, because in the coming Sections, we'll dive into each of these concepts in more detail, with practical examples and applications in data science.

It's important to understand that the power of linear algebra comes from its ability to efficiently represent and manipulate data, especially high-dimensional data. It forms the backbone of many data science operations and machine learning algorithms. While the depth of your required knowledge will depend on your specific role and tasks in data science, a solid foundation in linear algebra will undoubtedly empower you to better understand and implement data science solutions.

As we delve deeper into the mathematical wonderland that underpins data science, remember that our goal isn't to become professional mathematicians. Rather, it's to understand the key ideas and tools that can help us wrangle, analyze, and extract insights from data.

Linear algebra, with its vectors, matrices, and intricate operations, isn't just a field of abstract mathematics. It's a language that lets us communicate with data, understand its intricacies, and unlock its secrets.

probability and statistics

We've ventured through various territories in this fascinating landscape, and now we stand at the doorstep of two more fundamental domains - probability and statistics. Let's unravel their mysteries and discover their indispensable roles in data science.

. . .

First, let's tackle probability. At its core, probability is about quantifying the uncertainty associated with events chosen from a some universe of events. It's the math of chance and randomness. You've likely encountered this in everyday life, perhaps without even knowing it. Ever checked the weather forecast to decide if you need an umbrella? Or tried to figure out the best strategy to win a game? That's probability in action!

In data science, understanding probability can help us make predictions, model complex systems, and even quantify our confidence in certain outcomes. For instance, if you're building a model to predict whether an email is spam or not, probability can quantify how sure we are about our prediction. Concepts like random variables, probability distributions, and Bayes' theorem are key elements of this domain, and we'll explore each of these in-depth in our journey.

Next on our tour is the realm of statistics. If probability gives us the tools to predict the future based on our current data, statistics allows us to look at past data and make inferences about the larger world. In essence, statistics is about finding patterns in data and making decisions in the face of uncertainty.

As a data scientist, you'll often be in situations where you need to make decisions based on incomplete data. Here's where statistics comes in. It gives you methods to test your hypothesis, understand the relationship between different variables, and draw conclusions from data samples to larger populations.

Central to statistics is the concept of a statistical model – a mathematical representation of data. Models can range from simple linear regression, which predicts a response based on a single predictor, to complex deep learning models, which can handle large, complex datasets.

A key concept in statistics is the difference between descriptive and inferential statistics. Descriptive statistics summarize and organize characteristics of a data set, a necessary first step in understanding any new data. Inferential statistics, on the other hand, allows us to make claims or conclusions about the data based on a sample.

.   .   .

No statistical analysis is complete without a discussion on significance and p-values. These concepts help us determine whether the results we see in our sample data are due to chance or if they represent a significant trend. We'll delve into these ideas further, ensuring you have a robust understanding to inform your data analysis.

Both probability and statistics, each with their unique features, serve as powerful tools for data scientists. They provide the framework for interpreting, understanding, and predicting data. Whether you're testing a new feature for your website, making predictions about customer behavior, or interpreting results from a machine learning model, you'll be drawing on principles from both of these disciplines.

calculus

We've ventured into the realms of Linear Algebra, Probability, and Statistics. Now, it's time to embark on a new journey into a critical and fascinating realm of mathematics: Calculus.

.   .   .

Calculus might evoke memories of high school math class, filled with complex equations and intricate graphs. But in the world of data science, calculus is less about the minutiae of solving complex equations, and more about understanding changes, trends, and the nature of functions – the fundamental principles that drive many data science algorithms and models.

In the simplest of terms, calculus is the study of how things change. It's the language of motion, growth, and change. And what's more dynamic and changeable than the ever-evolving streams of data we work with in data science?

The first big idea in calculus is the concept of a derivative. If you have a function that describes how something changes—say, how a company's profits change over time—the derivative of that function gives you the rate of change at any given point. In other words, it's a measure of how a function is sloping or curving. In machine learning, this concept is critical for optimization algorithms like gradient descent, where we iteratively adjust model parameters to minimize a cost function.

. . .

The second key idea in calculus is the integral. While a derivative measures the rate of change, the integral, in contrast, measures the total accumulation of quantity over a specific interval. Think about the total sales over a given period, the total distance traveled, or the total number of website clicks. In data science, integration often comes up when we work with probabilities, helping us compute the total likelihood of certain outcomes.

To understand these concepts thoroughly, we need to consider limits. The idea of a limit lets us formalize the notion of a 'tiny change,' which underpins both derivatives and integrals. It's the idea of getting 'infinitesimally close' to a particular value. Though this might sound abstract, it's a crucial foundation for many of the calculations in calculus.

Now, why does all of this matter to data science? In machine learning, we're often looking to optimize some objective - for example, finding the best parameters that minimize prediction error. Calculus, especially the concept of a derivative, provides a way to do this efficiently. Without calculus, optimizing a machine learning model would be a much more challenging and computationally intensive process.

Calculus also gives us the tools to understand and interpret machine learning models. By understanding the cost function's shape and how it changes, we can gain insights into our model's learning process, diagnose issues, and even improve its performance.

While calculus can seem intimidating at first, remember, our goal isn't to become expert mathematicians. It's to understand the fundamental ideas and how they apply to data science. This understanding will allow us to use existing tools and software more effectively, diagnose and solve problems, and even communicate our results more clearly.

introduction to programming

understanding the basics of programming

WE'VE NAVIGATED the mathematical landscapes of Linear Algebra, Probability, Statistics, and Calculus, laying a robust foundation for our data science journey. Now, it's time to introduce another critical component of a data scientist's toolkit: Programming.

Don't worry if you've never written a line of code before, or if the thought of programming seems daunting. We'll start from the basics and build up your skills one step at a time. The aim isn't to turn you into a full-blown software developer, but to equip you with the coding skills needed to handle data effectively, perform analysis, and develop models.

Let's start by answering a fundamental question:

What is programming? Programming, at its core, is a way of instructing a computer to perform specific tasks. These instructions are written in a language that the computer can understand – hence the term 'programming language'. The art of programming involves designing, writing, testing, debugging, and maintaining these instructions to achieve your desired outcome.

An essential aspect of programming is understanding algorithms. An algorithm is a step-by-step process to solve a particular problem. Think of it as a recipe for getting from problem to solution. Algorithms form the backbone of any program and play a crucial role in data science. They are at the heart of everything from sorting data to implementing machine learning models.

Control structures, like loops and conditional statements, are another fundamental programming concept. Loops allow us to perform a task multiple times, which can be especially useful when working with large datasets. Conditional statements, on the other hand, let our program make decisions based on certain criteria. For example, a machine learning model might predict whether an email is spam or not based on certain characteristics.

Next comes understanding functions. Functions are blocks of code designed to perform a specific task, and they can be reused throughout your program. Functions in programming are somewhat analogous to functions in mathematics. Just like a mathematical function takes an input, performs an operation, and returns an output, a programming function works in a similar way.

An important aspect of modern programming, especially in data science, is the use of libraries or packages. These are collections of pre-written code that we can use to perform common tasks without having to code everything from scratch. Python, a popular language in data science, has a rich ecosystem of libraries like NumPy for numerical computing, Pandas for data manipulation, Matplotlib for data visualization, and Scikit-learn for machine learning.

One more crucial concept is understanding data structures. Data structures are specific ways of organizing and storing data in a computer so that it can be used efficiently. Some basic types of data structures include arrays, lists, and dictionaries. Mastering these will help you manipulate, analyze, and visualize data more effectively.

Now, let's pause and consider the big picture. You might be wondering, why is programming so important in data science? The answer is simple: it provides the tools to transform raw data into meaningful insights. With programming, we can automate data collection, clean and process large datasets, perform complex mathematical calculations, visualize trends and patterns, and build predictive models.

As we venture deeper into the realm of programming, remember that the goal is to learn how to express your ideas and solve problems in a way a computer can understand. We'll focus on practical programming skills specifically tailored to data science tasks, rather than trying to cover every aspect of computer science.

Learning to program is like learning a new language. It may feel unfamiliar and challenging at first, but with practice, you'll become more fluent and start to see the powerful possibilities it opens up. It's an essential tool for any data scientist and a gateway to unlocking the full potential of data.

introduction to python: the preferred language of data science

Python, named not after the snake but after the British comedy troupe Monty Python, is a high-level, interpreted programming language known for its simplicity and readability. It has become one of the most popular languages for data science, thanks to its ease of learning, extensive libraries, and supportive community.

Python is sometimes referred to as "executable

pseudocode," which is a fancy way of saying it's designed to be easy to read and write. The syntax - that's the set of rules that dictate how programs written in a language must be structured - is clean and straightforward. If you've never programmed before, Python is a fantastic place to start.

For data science, one of Python's biggest strengths is its rich ecosystem of libraries specifically designed for data analysis, visualization, and machine learning. These libraries are collections of code written by others that we can use to perform common tasks, saving us the time and effort of having to write these functions ourselves.

Pandas, for example, provides data structures and functions needed for manipulating and analyzing structured data. NumPy is indispensable for numerical computing, providing support for arrays and a plethora of mathematical functions. Matplotlib and Seaborn are excellent for data visualization, while Scikit-learn and TensorFlow provide tools for machine learning and artificial intelligence.

But Python isn't just for beginners or those focusing on data analysis. It's also widely used in web development, software development, artificial intelligence, and many other areas of programming. This versatility means that learning Python not only equips you with a powerful tool for data science but also opens doors to many other fields.

In our exploration of Python, we'll start by mastering the basics. This includes understanding data types like integers, floats, strings, and booleans, and how to work with them. We'll also delve into data structures such as lists, dictionaries, and sets.

We'll cover control structures like 'if', 'for', and 'while', and learn how to define and use functions. We'll explore how to handle errors and exceptions, a crucial aspect of writing robust, reliable code. And of course, we'll get hands-on practice with Python's powerful libraries for data analysis and visualization.

As we progress, we'll also touch on some best practices in Python programming. These include writing clean, readable code; commenting and documenting your work; and using version control systems like Git, which allow you to track changes to your code, collaborate with others, and manage your projects effectively.

Remember, the key to mastering Python, like any other skill, is practice. Don't be afraid to get your hands dirty with code. Experiment, make mistakes, learn from them, and keep going. And don't worry if things don't make sense at first - programming is a bit like a puzzle, and sometimes it takes time for the pieces to fall into place.

As we embark on our Python journey, let's remember that we're not just learning a programming language. We're gaining a powerful tool to express our ideas, solve problems, and bring our data to life. With Python in our toolkit, we're well-equipped to tackle the challenges and opportunities that lie ahead in our data science journey.

basic python for data science: libraries and tools

As we continue our adventure into the world of data science, we're about to delve deeper into the Python programming language. Specifically, we'll explore some of the most essential libraries and tools that make Python such a versatile choice for data science.

Python's strength for data science lies not just in its readability and simplicity, but also in its expansive ecosystem of libraries - prepackaged collections of code that perform common tasks. We can think of these libraries as toolkits, each filled with a unique set of tools designed to solve a particular set of problems. The right toolkit can make our work faster, easier, and more effective.

Firstly, let's talk about Pandas. Pandas is one of the most popular Python libraries for data manipulation and analysis. It introduces two powerful data structures: the DataFrame and the Series. A DataFrame is a two-dimensional labeled data structure, similar to a table in a relational database, an Excel spreadsheet, or a data frame in R. A Series, on the other hand, is a one-dimensional labeled array capable of holding any data type. With Pandas, we can perform tasks like handling missing data, merging and reshaping datasets, and applying mathematical operations across entire columns of data.

Next up is NumPy, short for 'Numerical Python'. NumPy is a library designed for scientific computing. It provides a high-performance multidimensional array object and tools for working with these arrays. It's particularly useful for mathematical tasks like generating random numbers, performing statistical operations, and applying mathematical functions on arrays.

For data visualization, we have Matplotlib and Seaborn. Matplotlib is a powerful library for creating static, interactive, and animated visualizations in Python. Seaborn, which is built on top of Matplotlib, provides a high-level interface for creating attractive statistical graphics. With these tools, we can transform our data into meaningful visual narratives, helping us and others understand the patterns and relationships within the data.

For machine learning, there's Scikit-learn. Scikit-learn is an open-source library that provides simple and efficient tools for predictive data analysis. It's built on NumPy, SciPy, and Matplotlib, and it offers tools for tasks like regression, classification, clustering, and dimensionality reduction.

TensorFlow, another library for machine learning, is a bit more advanced. Developed by Google Brain, TensorFlow is an open-source library for numerical computation and large-scale machine learning. It uses data flow graphs where nodes represent mathematical operations, while the edges represent the data arrays (tensors) communicated between them.

Aside from libraries, Python also offers several tools that make the development process smoother. Jupyter Notebooks, for instance, are a web-based interactive computational environment where you can combine code execution, rich text, mathematics, plots, and rich media. They're a great tool for data cleaning and transformation, numerical simulation, statistical modeling, data visualization, and machine learning.

Lastly, let's not forget about IDEs, or Integrated Development Environments. These are software applications that provide comprehensive facilities to computer programmers for software development. Popular Python IDEs include PyCharm and Spyder. These IDEs offer features like code suggestions, debugging tools, and integrations with version control systems like Git.

We've covered quite a bit, but this is just the tip of the iceberg! Python's ecosystem is vast and continually evolving, with libraries and tools for virtually every aspect of data science.

As we delve deeper into these libraries in the coming Sections, remember that they're here to help us. They're our tools, designed to make our lives as data scientists easier and more productive. Embrace them, learn to use them well, and they'll be invaluable allies on our data science journey.

3 /
data analysis and
visualization

understanding data analysis

YOU'RE NOW well-versed with Python, its libraries, and tools. It's time we approach an integral part of our journey: data analysis.

Data analysis is the heart of data science. It's the process where we make sense of data, find patterns, derive insights, and ultimately, create value. It can be like solving a complex puzzle, except the pieces are the bits and bytes of data we collect, and the final picture is the valuable insight we seek.

Data analysis is broadly classified into two types: qualitative and quantitative. Qualitative analysis involves assessing the qualities of the data, like themes or concepts. This might include categories, patterns, or trends that emerge from the data. On the other hand, quantitative analysis involves numerical data and statistical techniques to understand the data's quantities, frequencies, and patterns.

In data science, the steps we typically follow in data analysis include data cleaning, data exploration, data visualization, and interpretation. Let's break these down.

First is data cleaning, sometimes called data munging or wrangling. In the real world, data is often messy, inconsistent, or missing altogether. Data cleaning is about getting the data into a form where it can be worked with. It includes handling missing values, correcting inconsistencies, and creating a consistent format. Python's Pandas library, which we've discussed, is a powerful tool for data cleaning.

Next is data exploration, or exploratory data analysis (EDA). This is where we get to know our data, seeking to understand its main characteristics and structure. It involves calculating statistics, like mean and median, and understanding distributions. It might also involve seeking relationships between variables, or looking for outliers. Python's NumPy and SciPy libraries are commonly used for EDA.

Then comes data visualization, a crucial step in data analysis. Visualization transforms complex data into intuitive, easy-to-understand graphical representations. This can help both you and others understand the data, identify trends and outliers, and communicate findings. For data visualization, Python's Matplotlib and Seaborn libraries are your go-to tools.

Finally, we have the interpretation of results. This is where we make sense of everything we've discovered. It's where we answer the questions we set out to solve and potentially pose new questions based on our findings.

As we learn data analysis, one thing to keep in mind is the importance of critical thinking. Data analysis isn't just about performing computations or making charts. It's about asking the right questions, making informed judgments, and being aware of the limitations and potential biases in our data and our analysis.

Remember, data doesn't speak for itself. It's our interpretation of data that provides insights and drives decision-making. And these interpretations should always be driven by a thorough, well-executed analysis.

tools and techniques for data visualization

A well-crafted visualization can communicate complex data in a straightforward, easily digestible manner. It can reveal patterns, relationships, and trends that might otherwise go unnoticed. More than that, effective data visualization can tell a story, transforming raw numbers into a narrative that can inform, persuade, and inspire.

When it comes to tools for creating these visual narratives, Python offers an array of powerful libraries. You're already familiar with a few of these from our previous Sections: Matplotlib and Seaborn.

Matplotlib is the granddaddy of Python visualization libraries. It's versatile, powerful, and highly customizable, making it suitable for generating all kinds of static, animated, and interactive plots. Line plots, scatter plots, bar plots, histograms—you name it, Matplotlib can create it. While it may take a bit more code to create a plot in Matplotlib compared to some other libraries, the tradeoff is a high degree of control over every aspect of the visualization.

Seaborn builds on Matplotlib by providing a higher-level interface for creating statistical graphics. It comes with several built-in themes that beautify Matplotlib plots and adds some useful functions for creating complex plot types. Its primary strength is producing plots that represent statistical relationships among variables, like heat maps, pair plots, and facet grids.

Another exciting library to consider is Plotly. Plotly is a multi-language tool that allows for interactive and browser-based plots. The ability to hover over points, zoom in, and manipulate views can provide a more immersive and engaging experience. It's a go-to tool when you need to create interactive plots for the web.

Bokeh, like Plotly, is another library for creating interactive and dynamic visualizations. It shines in creating complex dashboard-style visualizations and is a popular choice among financial analysts for its powerful time-series capabilities.

The selection of a library will often depend on the specific needs of your project—whether you need static or interactive plots, the complexity of your visualization, and your personal preference.

Beyond these libraries, there are also several essential techniques and best practices in data visualization to keep in mind. Firstly, always know your audience. The design choices you make should depend on who will be consuming your visualizations and what their existing knowledge and expectations are.

Next, prioritize clarity and simplicity. It can be tempting to make a chart with a lot of colors, fancy font, or complex design elements, but these can often distract from the data. The best visualizations are often the simplest.

Moreover, always label your charts clearly. This includes the title, axis labels, and legend. A visualization should be able to stand on its own without needing additional explanation.

Also, remember to consider scale and context. A chart can be misleading if the scale is skewed or if the data lacks the necessary context for understanding.

Lastly, be ethical. Misrepresenting data, even unintentionally, can lead to false conclusions and decisions based on those conclusions. Always strive to represent your data truthfully and responsibly.

The world of data visualization is a combination of art and science. It requires both a creative eye for aesthetics and a logical mind for data interpretation. In the upcoming Sections, we'll explore in more detail how to leverage the power of Python libraries to create meaningful and impactful visualizations.

hands-on: analyzing and visualizing data with python

You've now gathered a wealth of knowledge about Python, data analysis, and visualization. It's time to put these concepts into practice and embark on a hands-on journey through a real-world data analysis and visualization project. Are you ready? Let's dive in!

First off, we need some data to work with. For this exercise, let's use a public dataset: the Iris dataset. This classic dataset includes measurements of 150 iris flowers from three different species. It's small and simple, but it gives us plenty to explore. You can find it readily available in several Python libraries, such as seaborn or sklearn, or you can download it from the UCI Machine Learning Repository.

Let's start by loading the data using seaborn and examining the first few rows:

```python
import seaborn as sns
# Load iris dataset
iris = sns.load_dataset('iris')
# Display first five rows
print(iris.head())
```

The dataset has five columns: 'sepal_length', 'sepal_width', 'petal_length', 'petal_width', and 'species'. The first four are numerical measurements in centimeters, and 'species' is a categorical variable representing the species of the iris.

Next, let's do some basic exploratory data analysis. We can use Pandas to generate some summary statistics:

```python
# Summary statistics
print(iris.describe())
```

This will provide us with the count, mean, standard

deviation, minimum, 25th percentile, median (50th percentile), 75th percentile, and maximum for each numerical column in the dataframe.

Now, let's dive a bit deeper and visualize our data. We'll use seaborn to create a pairplot, which will show us the distribution of each measurement, as well as scatterplots comparing every pair of measurements:

```python
# Pairplot
sns.pairplot(iris, hue='species')
```

This plot can help us see relationships between variables and how these relationships differ by species. Do you notice anything interesting?

At this point, you might want to explore other types of visualizations. Try creating a histogram of one variable, a boxplot comparing one variable across species, or a correlation heatmap of all the numerical variables.

Finally, it's time to interpret our findings. What have we learned from our analysis? How do the measurements vary between species? Are there any patterns, relationships, or outliers that stand out? Remember, this is where your critical thinking skills come into play. It's not just about what the data says, but what it means.

To wrap up this hands-on project, let's reflect on the process. What did you find challenging? What did you learn? How might you approach a similar project in the future? Remember, like any skill, data analysis and visualization take practice. The more you do it, the more comfortable and proficient you'll become.

We've taken an exciting step today, transforming theoretical knowledge into practical skill. And remember, this is just the beginning. With these foundational skills, you're well on your way to tackling more complex and challenging data projects.

4 /

databases and sql for data science

understanding databases: sql vs nosql

HAVING VENTURED into the practical realm of data analysis and visualization, let's shift our gears towards an essential aspect of data management – databases. Our main focus today is the classic conundrum: SQL or NoSQL?

So what is a database? In the simplest terms, a database is a structured set of data. It's like a massive, highly organized digital filing system where information is stored, managed, and retrieved. The efficiency and effectiveness of data management can make or break a data-driven project, hence the importance of understanding databases.

Now, databases can be broadly categorized into two types: SQL and NoSQL. SQL, or Structured Query

Language, databases have been around since the 1970s. They use a structured language to manage data stored in a relational model. Conversely, NoSQL databases, a newer breed, are non-relational and can handle unstructured data.

Let's delve a little deeper into each of these database types, starting with SQL.

SQL Databases

SQL databases, also known as relational databases, organize data into one or more tables. Each table is similar to an Excel spreadsheet, with rows and columns. The columns represent different attributes, and the rows represent individual records. Tables are linked to each other through keys, forming relationships between different data points. This organized structure allows SQL databases to handle complex queries efficiently.

Common examples of SQL databases include MySQL, Oracle, PostgreSQL, and SQLite. A major benefit of SQL databases is their ACID compliance (Atomicity, Consistency, Isolation, Durability), ensuring reliable processing of database transactions.

The structured nature of SQL databases, however, can be a double-edged sword. While it promotes data consistency and integrity, it might be less flexible when dealing with hierarchical or multi-valued data.

NoSQL Databases

The term NoSQL stands for "Not Only SQL". As this name suggests, NoSQL databases are a reaction to SQL databases' limitations. They handle the growing need to store and manipulate unstructured data such as social media posts, user-generated content, sensor data, and more.

NoSQL databases are schema-less, meaning they don't require a fixed structure like SQL databases. Instead, they offer flexibility, allowing fields to be added on the fly and each 'row' or 'record' to have a unique set of fields.

NoSQL databases come in various types, including document databases (like MongoDB), key-value stores (like Redis), wide-column stores (like Cassandra), and graph databases (like Neo4j). They shine in scenarios involving big data, real-time web applications, and distributed computing.

However, NoSQL databases trade some ACID properties for flexibility and performance, which can potentially lead to data inconsistencies.

SQL vs NoSQL: Which one to choose?

The answer, as you might have guessed, is: it depends. The choice between SQL and NoSQL is not about which one is better, but rather about which one is better suited to a particular project's needs.

If you have structured data with clear relations and need to perform complex queries, an SQL database could be your best bet. SQL databases are also a good fit for projects requiring transactional reliability, such as financial systems.

On the other hand, if you're dealing with massive amounts of unstructured data, or if your data requirements are rapidly evolving, a NoSQL database might serve you better. They are particularly useful for cloud-based storage, real-time applications, and handling big data.

As you continue your journey as a data scientist, you'll likely encounter both SQL and NoSQL databases. Understanding the strengths and weaknesses of each type will enable you to make informed decisions about the right tool for your task.

basics of sql for data science

As we noted in our previous Section, understanding databases is crucial for any data scientist, and SQL is a big part of that story.

SQL, which stands for Structured Query Language, is the standard language for dealing with relational databases. Whether you're dealing with MySQL, PostgreSQL, Oracle, or another relational database management system (RDBMS), SQL is the common tongue they all understand. Now, let's get our hands dirty and dive into the basics.

The Structure of SQL

SQL can be used for a variety of tasks, including querying data, updating data, creating and modifying database structures, and controlling access to data. However, we'll start with the most fundamental operation: querying data, which is achieved using the SELECT statement.

A basic SELECT statement includes the following:

```sql
SELECT column_name
FROM table_name;
```

This command retrieves data from a single column of a table. If you want to select multiple columns, you separate them with commas:

```sql
SELECT column1_name, column2_name
FROM table_name;
```

And if you want to select all columns, you can use an asterisk (*):

```sql
SELECT *
FROM table_name;
```

Filtering Rows with WHERE

Sometimes you'll want to retrieve data that meets

certain conditions. This is where the WHERE clause comes in. Here's an example:

```sql
SELECT *
FROM table_name
WHERE column_name = 'Value';
```

You can use various operators in your WHERE clause, including equals (=), not equals (<> or !=), less than (<), greater than (>), less than or equal to (<=), greater than or equal to (>=), BETWEEN, LIKE, and IN.

Sorting Results with ORDER BY

If you want to sort your results, you can use the ORDER BY clause:

```sql
SELECT *
FROM table_name
ORDER BY column_name ASC; -- for ascending order
```

Or:

```sql
SELECT *
FROM table_name
ORDER BY column_name DESC; -- for descending order
```

Joining Tables

One of the strengths of SQL and relational databases is the ability to combine data from different tables. This is done through JOIN operations. The most common type is the INNER JOIN:

```sql
SELECT          Orders.OrderID,          Customers.CustomerName
FROM Orders
INNER JOIN Customers
ON Orders.CustomerID = Customers.CustomerID;
```

This statement would return a table with the OrderID from the Orders table and the CustomerName from the Customers table, where the CustomerID matches in both tables.

SQL offers other types of joins as well, such as LEFT JOIN, RIGHT JOIN, and FULL JOIN, each serving different purposes.

Aggregating Data

Finally, SQL provides functions to aggregate data, such as COUNT(), SUM(), AVG(), MAX(), and MIN(). These functions can be used in conjunction with the GROUP BY clause:

```sql
SELECT COUNT(OrderID), CustomerID
FROM Orders
```

    GROUP BY CustomerID;
    ```

This statement returns the number of orders each customer has made.

That's just a taste of SQL's capabilities, but these basic concepts form the foundation of much of what you'll do with SQL as a data scientist.

Moving forward, keep in mind that SQL is a powerful and flexible tool in your data science toolkit. Its universality and depth make it an essential skill to master. But don't be daunted – with practice, you'll find it to be a reliable companion in your data exploration adventures.

# working with large datasets

As a data scientist, you will often find yourself working with massive amounts of data, sometimes running into gigabytes or even terabytes. This Section aims to equip you with the strategies and tools necessary for handling such datasets effectively.

### Understanding the Challenges of Large Datasets

Working with large datasets, often referred to as big data, brings unique challenges. The sheer size of the data can cause problems with storage, processing speed, and memory. You might find your scripts
    ```

running unbearably slow or even crashing due to memory overflow.

While it might be tempting to just upgrade your hardware, often that's a costly solution and doesn't address the root problem – inefficient data processing. Let's discuss some strategies that can help overcome these issues without breaking the bank.

Sampling Data

When your dataset is so big that it's unwieldy, one viable strategy is to work with a sample of your data. Sampling allows you to work with a manageable subset of data while maintaining statistical significance. This strategy can help you develop and test your data processing scripts without getting bogged down by the size of your data.

Remember, sampling isn't about choosing random data points. It's about selecting a representative subset of your data that can help you make inferences about the whole dataset.

Using Efficient Data Structures

The way you store your data in memory can have a significant impact on performance. Using efficient data structures can help reduce memory usage and improve processing speed.

For instance, in Python, Pandas DataFrames are often used for data manipulation. However, they can be memory-intensive. If you're dealing with large datasets, you might consider using Dask, a parallel computing library that extends Pandas to handle larger-than-memory computations. Dask can work on datasets that don't fit into memory by breaking them into smaller chunks and processing these chunks in a parallel manner.

Optimizing Code

While handling large datasets, it's crucial to write optimized code. Avoid loops whenever possible as they can be very slow on large datasets. Instead, use vectorized operations, which are typically faster as they leverage low-level optimizations.

Also, remember that not all functions are created equal. Some functions may run faster than others for the same task. For instance, in Python, the `map()` function is often faster than `apply()`.

Using Big Data Tools

Sometimes, your dataset may be so large that even the above strategies won't suffice. In such cases, you may need to resort to big data tools designed specifically for processing large datasets. These tools use techniques like parallel processing, distributed computing, and lazy evaluation to handle big data efficiently.

Apache Spark is one such tool that's widely used in the data science industry. It's an open-source, distributed computing system that can process large datasets in parallel across a cluster of computers. Spark has APIs for several programming languages, including Python and R, making it a convenient tool for data scientists.

Hadoop is another big data tool that you might come across. It's a framework that allows for the distributed processing of large datasets across clusters of computers using simple programming models. Hadoop, however, has a steeper learning curve and is typically used by data engineers.

Scaling with Cloud Services

Cloud computing services like Amazon AWS, Google Cloud, and Microsoft Azure also provide solutions for handling big data. These platforms offer scalable storage and computing power, meaning you can adjust resources based on your needs. They also provide various big data tools, including managed Hadoop and Spark services, which can simplify your big data processing tasks.

Working with large datasets can initially seem daunting, but with the right strategies and tools, it's a manageable task. Remember, handling big data is a fundamental part of being a data scientist. The ability to manipulate and extract insights from large datasets can distinguish you as a data scientist and open up new opportunities.

5 /
data cleaning and
preprocessing

the importance of clean and organized data

LET'S embark on a journey to the heart of the data science process—cleaning and organizing data. It may not sound as exciting as machine learning or big data, but it's just as important. If not more. After all, the conclusions you draw and predictions you make are only as good as the data you start with.

Understanding the Data Landscape

Data is everywhere, collected from a variety of sources, in different formats, and with varying levels of accuracy. Data can be numerical, categorical, text, images, or even audio. But no matter the type, data rarely comes to us in a neat package, ready for analysis.

More often, it's messy, unorganized, and riddled with inaccuracies.

What is Clean and Organized Data?

Clean data, in essence, is accurate, complete, and formatted correctly. Cleaning data involves correcting or removing any inaccuracies or discrepancies that could skew your results or lead to incorrect conclusions. Examples of dirty data might include typos in text data, incorrect numeric entries, or missing values.

Organized data, on the other hand, is structured in a way that optimizes it for your specific analyses. This could mean aggregating data, restructuring tables, or creating new variables. The goal of organizing your data is to streamline your analyses and make your data easier to work with.

Why is Clean and Organized Data Important?

Think of your data as the ingredients for a meal. If you start with spoiled ingredients, no amount of culinary skill can save your dish. The same applies to data. If you start with inaccurate or disorganized data, your results will be skewed, potentially leading you to incorrect conclusions. Cleaning and organizing your data ensures that your analyses are built on a solid foundation.

But there's more to it than just accuracy. Clean and organized data can also save you time. Have you ever tried finding something in a messy room? It's time-consuming and frustrating. The same principle applies to data. If your data is disorganized, you'll waste valuable time trying to find what you need or correcting mistakes.

How to Clean and Organize Data

Cleaning and organizing data is a multifaceted process and can involve a variety of techniques. For numerical data, you might need to correct outliers or fill in missing values. For categorical data, you might need to consolidate categories or correct spelling mistakes. The specific techniques will depend on your data and your analysis goals.

A good first step in any data cleaning process is to understand your data. This means looking at your data, summarizing it, and identifying potential problems. This exploratory data analysis (EDA) is crucial in identifying areas where your data may need cleaning.

Once you've identified the problems, you can start cleaning your data. This can involve a variety of techniques, from simple things like removing duplicates or filling missing values to more complex tasks like correcting inconsistencies or dealing with outliers.

After your data is clean, you can start organizing it. This might involve restructuring your data, creating new variables, or aggregating data. The goal is to create a dataset that is easy to work with and optimized for your specific analysis.

Tools for Cleaning and Organizing Data

There are many tools available for cleaning and organizing data. Python, for example, has several libraries that can help with this process, including Pandas, NumPy, and Scikit-learn. These libraries offer functions for handling missing data, correcting outliers, encoding categorical variables, and more.

SQL can also be used for data cleaning and organization. It offers commands for filtering data, dealing with null values, and restructuring tables. While SQL is not as flexible as Python for data cleaning, it can be very effective, especially when working with large databases.

The Hidden Value in Cleaning and Organizing Data

Lastly, it's worth noting that cleaning and organizing data isn't just a chore—it's an opportunity. Each time you clean or organize a dataset, you learn more about that data. You might discover patterns, identify potential problems, or uncover valuable insights. So while it might be tempting to rush through this step, take your time. You never know what you might find.

We've covered a lot of ground in this Section, highlighting the crucial role that clean and organized data plays in data science. From the repercussions of dirty data to the process and tools for cleaning and organizing data, I hope you now appreciate the importance of this often overlooked aspect of the data science process.

techniques for data cleaning

It's time to roll up our sleeves and delve deeper into the nitty-gritty of data cleaning. In the last Section, we talked about the importance of clean and organized data, and now, we're going to learn the techniques to achieve it.

Dealing with Missing Data

One of the most common problems you'll encounter in a dataset is missing data. Whether it's due to errors in data collection, issues with data transfer, or intentional omission, missing data can seriously affect your analysis.

One straightforward approach to handle missing data is to simply remove it. However, this method should be used judiciously, as it might result in loss of valuable information, especially if your dataset is small or the missing data is not randomly distributed.

Alternatively, you can fill in the missing data. Common filling methods include using a constant value, the mean, median or mode of the column, or using a predictive model to estimate the missing values. Remember, the best method to use depends on the nature of your data and the context of your analysis.

Handling Outliers

Outliers are data points that are significantly different from the rest of the data. While some outliers are genuine, others can be due to errors or anomalies in data collection.

Outliers can greatly impact your data analysis and predictive modeling if not properly handled. For instance, they can skew your data, leading to inaccurate conclusions.

There are several ways to detect outliers, including statistical methods such as Z-score or IQR, or visualization tools like box plots and scatter plots. Once detected, you can handle outliers by either removing them or transforming them, depending on whether they are genuine or not.

Correcting Inaccurate Data

Not all dirty data is missing or outlying—sometimes, it's just incorrect. For example, you might have a dataset of people's ages, but one entry says a person is 250 years old—a clear mistake.

Detecting inaccurate data can be challenging. One way to spot it is by knowing your data well, using your domain knowledge to identify things that don't make sense. Once identified, you can handle inaccurate data by correcting it (if you have the correct information), removing it, or flagging it as suspicious and investigating further.

Formatting Your Data Correctly

Data can come in a variety of formats, and incorrect or inconsistent formatting can make it hard to analyze your data. For instance, dates might be entered as MM-DD-YYYY in one column and DD-MM-YYYY in another. Inconsistent capitalization and spelling mistakes in categorical variables are other common issues.

Standardizing and formatting your data correctly makes it easier to work with and can help prevent errors in your analysis. This might involve converting data types, standardizing text entries, or restructuring your data.

Utilizing Python Libraries for Data Cleaning

Python, with its powerful libraries like Pandas, Numpy, and Scikit-learn, is an excellent tool for data cleaning. For instance, you can use the Pandas library to handle missing data, detect and handle outliers, and format your data. It provides functions to drop or fill missing values, identify duplicates, replace values, and much more.

To give you a quick example, in Pandas, if you wanted to fill missing values in your dataset with the mean, you could use the fillna() function like this:

```python
```

```
df = df.fillna(df.mean())
```

There, df is your DataFrame, and df.mean() calculates the mean of each column in your DataFrame. The fillna() function then replaces every missing value with the corresponding column's mean.

In this Section, we've explored a variety of techniques for cleaning data, from handling missing data and outliers to correcting inaccuracies

and formatting your data correctly. Armed with these techniques, you'll be well-prepared to tackle any dirty data that comes your way.

In the following Section, we'll go through some real-world examples and perform hands-on data cleaning using Python. Get ready to apply what you've learned to practical situations, because there's no better way to understand data cleaning than by actually doing it!

data preprocessing for machine learning

Data preprocessing is like the backstage crew at a play. While machine learning models (the actors) often get the spotlight, these models would be helpless without the meticulous preparation that goes on behind the scenes. In this Section, we're going to explore this critical process in depth.

What is Data Preprocessing?

Data preprocessing is the stage of preparing your raw data to be fed into a machine learning model. This involves several steps, including data cleaning (which we have already covered in previous Sections), data transformation, feature scaling, and data splitting. These steps aim to make the dataset more suitable for modeling, improving the performance and accuracy of the model.

Data Transformation

Transforming data involves changing the format, structure, or values of your data to make it more suitable for analysis. This could involve encoding categorical variables, feature engineering, or other transformations.

For instance, most machine learning algorithms require numerical input. If your dataset includes categorical variables, like 'color' with values 'red', 'blue', and 'green', you would need to encode these into numerical values, like 1, 2, and 3.

Feature engineering is another common form of data transformation. This involves creating new features from existing ones, for instance, by doing mathematical operations on features, grouping categories, or extracting information from dates. Good feature engineering can often improve the performance of your model significantly.

Feature Scaling

Feature scaling is a technique used to standardize the range of features in your dataset. Many machine learning algorithms perform better when all features are on a similar scale. This is because these algorithms use measures of distance between data points in their computations.

Two common methods of feature scaling are normalization and standardization. Normalization scales features to a range between 0 and 1, while standardization transforms features to have a mean of 0 and standard deviation of 1. The choice between these methods depends on your data and the algorithm you plan to use.

Data Splitting

Before you can train your model, you need to split your dataset into a training set and a test set. The training set is used to train the model, while the test set is used to evaluate the model's performance on unseen data. A common split is 80% of data for training and 20% for testing.

In Python, you can use the `train_test_split` function from the `sklearn.model_selection` module to do this. For example:

```python
```

```
from          sklearn.model_selection          import
train_test_split

X_train, X_test, y_train, y_test = train_test_split(X,
y, test_size=0.2, random_state=42)
```

Here, `X` is your set of features, and `y` is your target variable. The `test_size` parameter specifies the proportion of the data to be used for the test set.

Handling Imbalanced Data

In some datasets, you may find that your target variable's classes are not equally represented. This is known as an imbalanced dataset, and it can lead to biased models that favor the majority class.

There are several techniques to handle imbalanced data, including oversampling the minority class, undersampling the majority class, or using a combination of both (also known as SMOTE - Synthetic Minority Over-sampling Technique). The choice of technique depends on your specific dataset and problem.

Data preprocessing is a vital step in your machine learning project. As with cooking, the quality of your ingredients (data) profoundly affects the outcome of your dish (model).

6 /
understanding machine learning

supervised learning vs unsupervised learning

AS WE DELVE DEEPER into the fascinating world of machine learning, we come upon a critical crossroads: the distinction between supervised and unsupervised learning. To build effective machine learning models, understanding this difference is key. Let's unwrap these concepts and see how they influence our approach to problem-solving.

Understanding Supervised Learning

In supervised learning, we have a labeled dataset, which means we already know our target outcome. Think of it as a teacher-student scenario where the teacher (you) guides the student (the model) using a set of correct answers. Our model uses these answers to learn the relationships between the features and the target variable.

Two main types of supervised learning problems exist: regression and classification. In regression problems, the target variable is continuous, such as predicting the price of a house based on its features like size, location, and age. On the other hand, classification problems involve predicting discrete values, like whether an email is spam or not.

Python's `sklearn` library offers numerous algorithms for tackling supervised learning problems, including linear regression for regression problems, and decision trees, naive Bayes, and support vector machines for classification tasks.

Understanding Unsupervised Learning

Unsupervised learning, on the other hand, is more like exploratory learning. Here, the model is akin to a student studying on their own without any specific guidance. We provide it with an unlabeled dataset, and it discovers the underlying structure or patterns within the data.

Common unsupervised learning tasks include clustering and dimensionality reduction. Clustering involves grouping similar data points together, such as segmenting customers for targeted marketing campaigns. Dimensionality reduction is about simplifying data without losing too much information, which can be helpful when dealing with very high-dimensional data.

Algorithms used in unsupervised learning include K-means for clustering and Principal Component Analysis for dimensionality reduction.

The Difference Between Supervised and Unsupervised Learning

The fundamental difference between these two types of learning lies in the data they work with. Supervised learning requires a labeled dataset, meaning each data point includes a corresponding target value. Unsupervised learning, conversely, works with unlabeled data, seeking to uncover inherent structures or patterns.

The use cases for both types also differ. Supervised learning is typically used when we know what we're looking for, and we have past data that can guide the model. Unsupervised learning is used when we're not entirely sure what we're seeking or when we want the model to discover the answers on its own.

Choosing Between Supervised and Unsupervised Learning

The choice between supervised and unsupervised learning depends largely on your data and the problem you're trying to solve.

If you have labeled data and a specific prediction task, then supervised learning is usually the way to go.

It allows you to train a model that can make accurate predictions on new, unseen data.

However, if you don't have labels for your data or if you're interested in exploring your data to find patterns or structures, then unsupervised learning is a better choice. It can reveal insights that you might not find with supervised methods.

In reality, many machine learning projects may involve both types of learning. For instance, you could use unsupervised learning to explore and preprocess your data, then switch to supervised learning to build and evaluate your predictive model.

essential machine learning algorithms

Now that we've established a solid foundation in machine learning concepts, it's time to examine some of the most crucial algorithms in the field. These are the techniques that will enable you to extract valuable insights from your data. We'll explore five key types of algorithms: linear regression, logistic regression, decision trees, k-nearest neighbors, and k-means clustering. Let's get started!

Linear Regression

Linear regression is a fundamental algorithm in supervised learning, used for solving regression problems. It seeks to establish a linear relationship between the input variables (X) and a single output variable (Y). The algorithm assumes that Y can be represented as a linear combination of the input variables.

Linear regression works best when the variables are linearly dependent, that is, a change in one variable proportionately affects the change in another. It's popular in forecasting and trend analysis, like predicting housing prices or stock values.

Logistic Regression

Despite its name, logistic regression is used for binary classification problems, where the output is either 0 or 1. It applies the logistic function to a linear combination of features to predict the probability of a certain class. The result is a value between 0 and 1, which can be thresholded to predict a class directly.

Logistic regression is often used in scenarios where the outcome is binary, like predicting whether an email is spam or not, or diagnosing a disease as malignant or benign.

Decision Trees

A decision tree is another supervised learning algorithm that can be used for both classification and regression tasks. The model takes the form of a treelike structure, where each internal node represents a feature, each branch signifies a decision rule, and each leaf node denotes an outcome.

Decision trees are intuitive and easy to interpret,

which makes them great for visualizing the decision-making process. They are typically used in operations research, strategic planning, and advanced chess games.

K-Nearest Neighbors (K-NN)

K-Nearest Neighbors is an instance-based learning algorithm that is used for both classification and regression problems. The principle behind K-NN is simple: similar things are close to each other. The algorithm classifies a new instance based on the majority class of its 'k' nearest neighbors.

K-NN is considered a lazy learning method because it doesn't learn a discriminative function from the training data but memorizes the training dataset instead. It's used in recommendation systems, semantic searching, and anomaly detection.

K-Means Clustering

K-means is an unsupervised learning algorithm used for clustering problems. It works by partitioning the dataset into 'k' distinct, non-overlapping clusters. The algorithm tries to make the intra-cluster data points as similar as possible while also keeping the clusters as different (far) as possible.

K-means is used in various domains, including market segmentation, computer vision, geostatistics, and astronomy.

And there you have it - an overview of five essential machine learning algorithms. Each algorithm has its strengths and weaknesses, and the key to successful machine learning is to understand which algorithm to use when. It's also important to remember that the 'best' algorithm often depends on the size and nature of your data, the computational power you have at your disposal, and the problem you're trying to solve.

implementing machine learning algorithms in python

By now, you've been introduced to a handful of essential machine learning algorithms. You have a broad sense of what each algorithm does, and where it can be applied. This Section takes things a step further—we're going to dive into the practical side of things, exploring how to implement these algorithms in Python.

Python and Machine Learning

Python is the preferred language for many data scientists, and for good reason. Its simplicity and readability make it an excellent choice for beginners, while its powerful libraries—many of which were designed with data science in mind—make it a robust tool for experts. Today, we're going to leverage Python's Scikit-Learn library, a versatile tool for machine learning in Python.

Implementing Linear Regression

Our first task is implementing a linear regression model. Here's how we might tackle this in Python:

```python
from sklearn.linear_model import LinearRegression
model = LinearRegression()
model.fit(X_train, y_train)
predictions = model.predict(X_test)
```

In this example, 'X_train' and 'y_train' are our training data and labels, respectively. After we've fit the model, we can make predictions on our test data, 'X_test'.

Implementing Logistic Regression

Logistic regression is implemented in much the same way:

```python
from sklearn.linear_model import LogisticRegression
model = LogisticRegression()
model.fit(X_train, y_train)
predictions = model.predict(X_test)
```

Again, we fit the model with our training data and then make predictions on our test data.

Implementing Decision Trees

Decision Trees involve a similar procedure, with a different model:

```python
from sklearn.tree import DecisionTreeClassifier
model = DecisionTreeClassifier()
model.fit(X_train, y_train)
predictions = model.predict(X_test)
```

Note that DecisionTreeClassifier is used for classification tasks. For regression tasks, you would use DecisionTreeRegressor.

Implementing K-Nearest Neighbors

For the K-Nearest Neighbors algorithm, the process is similar, but we also specify the number of neighbors as an argument:

```python
from sklearn.neighbors import KNeighborsClassifier
model = KNeighborsClassifier(n_neighbors=3)
model.fit(X_train, y_train)
predictions = model.predict(X_test)
```

Remember that choosing the right value for 'k' is critical for the K-Nearest Neighbors algorithm.

Implementing K-Means Clustering

Lastly, K-Means is slightly different since it's an unsupervised learning algorithm:

```python
from sklearn.cluster import KMeans
```

```
model = KMeans(n_clusters=3)
model.fit(X)
predictions = model.predict(X)
```

Here, we're fitting the model and making predictions on the same dataset 'X', as we don't have labels in unsupervised learning.

deep learning and neural networks

introduction to neural networks

SO FAR IN THIS JOURNEY, we have dissected and played with some fundamental algorithms used in machine learning. Now, it's time to tackle an exciting and immensely popular area of data science - Neural Networks. If you've heard about artificial intelligence or deep learning, you've most certainly heard about Neural Networks.

The Inspiration Behind Neural Networks

The concept of neural networks isn't new—it originates from our endeavor to mimic the human brain's functioning. Our brain comprises billions of neurons that interact and transmit signals to perform an array of complex tasks. Inspired by this, computer scientists have developed Artificial Neural Networks (ANNs), mathematical models designed to mirror the structure and function of the human brain.

Artificial Neurons: The Building Blocks

The building blocks of ANNs are artificial neurons, or nodes. Each neuron receives one or more inputs, processes them, and produces an output. This operation isn't dissimilar to how biological neurons work.

In an artificial neuron, the inputs are numeric values, each multiplied by a corresponding weight. The neuron sums these weighted inputs and applies an activation function to the result, producing the output. The activation function determines the neuron's output based on its input—some activation functions, for example, allow only positive values to pass through.

Layering it up: The Network Structure

An Artificial Neural Network consists of multiple layers of these neurons—generally an input layer, an output layer, and one or more hidden layers in between. Each layer can contain any number of neurons. The hidden layers allow the network to learn complex patterns by creating new representations of the input data.

Learning in Neural Networks: The Backpropagation Algorithm

Neural networks learn through an algorithm called backpropagation. In simple terms, after making a prediction, the network calculates how far off it was from the actual result—this is the error. Backpropagation is then used to adjust the weights of the neurons, starting from the output layer and working back to the input layer, thus reducing the error. The process is repeated multiple times (epochs), further reducing the error each time.

What Makes Neural Networks Special?

Neural networks, especially deep ones with many layers, have proven exceptionally successful in many areas, such as image recognition, natural language processing, and complex game playing. They can capture complex patterns and create rich representations of data, outperforming other machine learning algorithms in certain tasks.

Potential Challenges

However, it's important to remember that neural networks also have their challenges. They can be computationally intensive, difficult to interpret, and prone to overfitting if not correctly regularized. Also, collecting the vast amounts of data required to train them can be a challenge.

Python and Neural Networks

Python offers powerful libraries for working with neural networks. TensorFlow, developed by Google Brain, and PyTorch, supported by Facebook's AI Research lab, are two prominent examples. Keras, a user-friendly neural-network library, runs on top of

TensorFlow, providing a simpler way to create and experiment with neural networks.

Neural Networks are just the Beginning

As you delve deeper into the world of data science, you'll discover more advanced types of neural networks, such as Convolutional Neural Networks (CNNs) used in image processing, and Recurrent Neural Networks (RNNs) used in sequence data like time series or text.

Stepping Forward

Neural networks represent an important leap in our journey. As the cornerstone of deep learning, understanding them can unlock many doors in the field of data science. They can seem intimidating at first, but once you start working with them, you'll see they're based on straightforward principles.

understanding convolutional neural networks

Now that we've laid the foundation by understanding basic neural networks, let's push the boundary further and step into the fascinating world of Convolutional Neural Networks, often abbreviated as CNNs.

Convolutional Neural Networks: A Special Type of Neural Network

CNNs are a special type of neural networks that

have proven incredibly successful in tasks involving image and video processing. You know the photo-tagging feature on social media platforms? That's CNNs in action!

The Concept of Convolution

The key concept that distinguishes CNNs is convolution. Convolution is a mathematical operation that involves the process of adding each element of the image to its local neighbors, weighted by the kernel (a small matrix).

This is akin to a flashlight being shone over the entire image, where the flashlight is the kernel, and the light falling on the image represents the operation of convolution. This "shining the flashlight" operation helps in highlighting features like edges, textures, or shapes—essentially, features that help us (and the machine) identify the image.

Structure of a CNN: The Convolutional Layer

CNNs typically consist of several types of layers, starting with the Convolutional Layer. This layer applies various filters to the input, each designed to recognize a specific feature in the image.

Each neuron in this layer is connected to only a small region of the input, and all neurons share the same weights and bias. This shared set of weights is called a filter or kernel, and it is moved over the input image to detect specific features.

The Pooling Layer: Simplifying Things

Following the convolutional layer, we often find the Pooling Layer. This layer's function is to progressively reduce the spatial size (width and height) of the input representation, making the computations more manageable. It works by summarizing the features present in the region of the image it is applied to, often taking the maximum value (Max Pooling) or the average value (Average Pooling).

Fully Connected Layer: Making Decisions

After several rounds of convolution and pooling, the high-level reasoning happens in the Fully Connected Layer. Neurons in this layer are connected to all activations in the previous layer, as seen in traditional Neural Networks. These layers might contain a Softmax activation function, which helps compute probabilities for each output class.

Training a CNN: Same Old Backpropagation

CNNs are trained through backpropagation, the same learning algorithm used for other neural networks. Given an input image, the CNN makes a prediction for the output. The error of this prediction is calculated using a loss function, and this error is then backpropagated through the network to adjust the weights.

Python and CNNs: Hello, TensorFlow and Keras

In Python, we can leverage powerful libraries to

work with CNNs. TensorFlow is a go-to option for high-performance tasks, while Keras, which runs on top of TensorFlow, is user-friendly and excellent for rapid experimentation.

CNNs and their Limitations

While CNNs are powerful for image analysis, they do have limitations. For example, they might struggle with understanding the context or sequence in images since they treat each image independently. For complex tasks like video processing or natural language processing, other types of neural networks, like Recurrent Neural Networks, might be more suitable.

Pushing the Envelope with CNNs

Remember, understanding CNNs can open up a wide array of possibilities in the data science realm, ranging from image classification, object detection, to even sophisticated self-driving car systems. The utility of CNNs extends to any task where pattern recognition in large datasets is required.

introduction to deep learning frameworks: tensorflow and pytorch

Now that we have our concepts clear about neural networks, convolutional neural networks, and the related mathematical jargon, we're ready to explore the practical side of implementing these concepts. Yes, we are talking about Deep Learning frameworks!

Deep Learning frameworks are the engines that power our ability to create artificial intelligence. These tools allow us to design, train, and validate deep neural networks, which are the core of modern AI applications. Today, we will discuss two of the most popular deep learning frameworks: TensorFlow and PyTorch.

TensorFlow: Google's Gift to AI Developers

TensorFlow is an open-source deep learning framework developed by Google's Brain Team. It was designed with one overarching goal in mind - to make it easier for developers to design, build, and train deep learning models.

At the heart of TensorFlow are Tensors - multi-dimensional arrays that you can think of as the building blocks of any data you might work with. The name "TensorFlow" stems from the operations which neural networks perform on these Tensors - essentially, the data "flows" through the model like water through a series of pipes.

TensorFlow is widely used in the industry and has strong support for production deployment, which means it's a great choice for building models that you might want to scale and serve to a large number of users. TensorFlow is also a vast ecosystem, not just a library to build and train neural networks. It comes with TensorFlow Lite for mobile and embedded systems, and TensorFlow Extended (TFX) for production-grade machine learning pipelines.

PyTorch: Facebook's Torchbearer in AI

PyTorch, on the other hand, is Facebook's offering in the world of deep learning. An open-source framework like TensorFlow, PyTorch is loved by researchers and developers alike for its simplicity and ease of use, especially when it comes to rapid prototyping.

While TensorFlow was explicitly designed for production, PyTorch was designed for the problem at hand - making research simpler. It features a dynamic computational graph, which allows for changes in the network structure in real-time, making it particularly suited for tasks that require frequent modifications and fine-tuning.

Its architecture allows you to see and work with gradients directly, which can be a boon when debugging your neural network. Unlike TensorFlow, where you define the entire computation graph before running your model, PyTorch allows you to define and manipulate your graph on-the-go.

TensorFlow vs. PyTorch: The Showdown

Choosing between TensorFlow and PyTorch might come down to your specific project needs, team skills, or simply personal preference. TensorFlow has been around for a while longer and is generally regarded as more mature for specific tasks and production-level applications. However, PyTorch, with its simplicity and flexibility, has been growing in popularity, especially in the research community.

But let's be clear - it's not a case of one being better than the other. They're both capable of achieving impressive results. It's more about understanding the strengths and weaknesses of each and using them to your advantage.

Stepping into Practicality with Python

Both TensorFlow and PyTorch offer Python-friendly interfaces, and in many ways, they have made deep learning accessible to the masses. With a clear, concise Python code, you can quickly design, train, and validate a wide array of deep learning models. With the help of TensorFlow's Keras or PyTorch's nn.Module, you can define complex architectures with just a few lines of code.

In the following Sections, we'll delve into the code, the architecture, and the nitty-gritty of working with both TensorFlow and PyTorch. We'll walk through practical examples, build out see how these frameworks bring our algorithms to life. We'll start by explaining the syntax, showing how to structure the code, and then dive into more complex concepts.

Ultimately, whether you choose to work with

TensorFlow or PyTorch, or perhaps both, knowing how to utilize these frameworks is a significant step forward on your data science journey. They are tools that offer a way to transform the theoretical knowledge of machine learning and deep learning into practical skills that can solve real-world problems. And remember, just like learning a new language, the more you practice using these frameworks, the more fluent you'll become.

8 /

natural language processing and computer vision

basics of natural language processing

WELCOME to the exciting world of Natural Language Processing (NLP), where we make computers understand and interpret human language. This remarkable field of data science is at the heart of many applications we use daily, from virtual assistants like Siri or Alexa to language translation services and sentiment analysis tools.

In essence, Natural Language Processing is a subfield of artificial intelligence that deals with the interaction between computers and humans using natural language. The goal is to enable computers to understand, interpret, and generate human language in a valuable way. It's about teaching our digital companions to understand us better, which, as you might guess, is not as straightforward as it sounds!

Why? Because human language is incredibly complex. It's filled with ambiguity, nuance, and intricacies, and varies greatly depending on context, culture, and personal experiences. Just think about slang words, idioms, or the different ways we can interpret a simple sentence based on the tone of voice or context.

To tackle this complexity, NLP uses various techniques and methodologies derived from several fields, including computer science, AI, and linguistics. These techniques enable the machine to convert human language into a format that it can understand, interpret and even generate responses that are meaningful to us.

One of the foundational aspects of NLP is text processing. Given that computers can't naturally understand human language, we need to convert text data into a format that a machine can understand - a process called text preprocessing. Text preprocessing involves several steps like tokenization (breaking down a sentence into individual words), stop-word removal (eliminating commonly used words like 'a', 'an', 'the'), stemming and lemmatization (reducing words to their root form), and encoding words as numerical vectors.

Another critical aspect is understanding the structure of sentences, a process called parsing. It involves analyzing a sentence to identify its grammatical components and how they're related. This can help determine the meaning of a sentence or whether it's grammatically correct.

As we progress, we will also introduce techniques like Named Entity Recognition (NER) which allows us to identify important elements like people, places, and organizations within a text, and sentiment analysis, which is used to determine the emotional tone behind words. These techniques help provide more context to the text data and thus aid in the understanding of human language.

Machine learning, specifically deep learning, has also significantly impacted NLP. With the introduction of models like Recurrent Neural Networks (RNN), Long Short Term Memory (LSTM) and, more recently, Transformer models like BERT (Bidirectional Encoder Representations from Transformers), NLP has seen substantial improvements in performance.

As we delve deeper into this Section, we will explore the essential concepts, methodologies, and tools in NLP, giving you a solid foundation to start implementing NLP in your projects.

Whether you're automating customer service with chatbots, analyzing social media sentiment, or creating a smart assistant, NLP will be an indispensable tool in your arsenal. So gear up, because we're about to dive headfirst into this fascinating world where linguistics, artificial intelligence, and data science converge!

understanding computer vision

Today, we're setting sail on the vast sea of computer vision, an extraordinary realm where computers gain high-level understanding from digital images or videos. It's a field where artificial intelligence mimics human vision, a field that's as exciting as it is transformative.

Computer vision sits at the intersection of mathematics, computer science, physics, and psychology. Its goal? To automate the tasks that the human visual system can do. The 'seeing' part is simple; after all, a camera connected to a computer can 'see'. The challenge is interpreting what it sees - understanding the content of an image or a video frame, recognizing patterns, and making sense of visual data in a fraction of a second.

In its essence, computer vision is teaching computers to 'see' and interpret the visual world. When you look at a group photo, for instance, you can immediately identify faces, tell who's happy or sad, or even guess where the photo was taken. That's a lot of processing and interpreting, something we humans do instinctively. For a computer, though, it's a much more complex task.

Why? Because images, for computers, are just arrays of pixel intensity values. A standard color image consists of red, green, and blue channels, each with pixel intensity values ranging from 0 to 255. When we talk about computer vision, we're talking about converting these pixel values into meaningful information.

Let's unpack that a bit. When we teach computers to interpret images, we're venturing into an array of fascinating tasks: object detection (locating and identifying multiple objects in an image), image segmentation (partitioning an image into multiple segments, or "pixels sets", often to locate objects and boundaries), face recognition, and even complex scene reconstruction.

This journey requires a deep dive into algorithms, from classic methods such as edge detection algorithms like Canny, to more modern, machine learning-based approaches including Convolutional Neural Networks (CNNs). We'll have to dip our toes into image classification, the foundation of computer vision, where we teach computers to categorize what they 'see' in an image.

Computer vision has practical applications that

touch virtually every aspect of our lives. Autonomous vehicles, for example, use computer vision for navigation and detecting objects. Medical imaging uses computer vision for detecting diseases and abnormalities. Even your smartphone camera uses computer vision for features like portrait mode and night mode!

The rising tide of deep learning has only pushed the field of computer vision further. Deep learning models, especially Convolutional Neural Networks (CNNs), have shown excellent performance in image classification tasks. Models like AlexNet, VGG, GoogLeNet, and ResNet have pushed the boundaries of what's possible and have achieved remarkable results in tasks like image classification, object detection, and semantic segmentation.

As we navigate through this Section, we'll dive into these exciting aspects, methodologies, and tools in computer vision. We'll take a look at the fundamental concepts of how images are stored and processed, the essential algorithms used in computer vision, and how we can harness the power of deep learning to process and understand visual data.

Of course, we will go beyond theory. We'll dip our oars into practical applications, helping you build a hands-on understanding of computer vision techniques.

real-world applications and examples

Buckle up, as we are about to embark on a journey to the real world where the magic of data science and artificial intelligence is transforming industries and shaping our lives in unimaginable ways. By applying what we've learned, we can make a substantial impact across numerous sectors. We'll explore some of the most prominent examples that illustrate this impact vividly.

Let's begin our exploration with healthcare, a sector that has seen some of the most profound impacts of data science and AI. For instance, imagine a system capable of predicting potential health issues based on one's medical history, genetic information, and lifestyle choices. It's not a pipe dream, but a reality that's improving lives and streamlining healthcare operations. AI-driven predictive analytics in healthcare not only enable early disease detection but also optimize the patient care process. For instance, machine learning algorithms can predict hospital readmission rates, helping healthcare providers to improve post-hospitalization care.

Venturing into the retail sector, you would find that companies are using data science for personalized marketing, inventory management, and customer sentiment analysis. Online retailers, for example, use recommendation systems that analyze customer browsing patterns and purchasing history to suggest products tailored to their preferences. These personalized recommendations drive customer engagement and significantly improve sales.

The transportation industry has seen a significant evolution thanks to data science. Autonomous vehicles, arguably the pinnacle of AI application, rely heavily on computer vision, a branch of AI that we discussed in detail in our previous Sections. In addition to that, ride-hailing services like Uber and Lyft use data science to calculate ETAs, surge pricing, and optimal routes, improving their service efficiency significantly.

In the domain of finance, AI and data science are playing critical roles in fraud detection, risk management, and customer service. Machine learning algorithms can detect patterns in vast datasets that human analysts might overlook, identifying fraudulent activities or pinpointing risk factors with far greater accuracy and speed.

The media and entertainment sector has been another significant beneficiary of data science and AI. Content streaming services like Netflix and Spotify use advanced recommendation systems to suggest movies or songs based on user behavior, enhancing user engagement. Even news agencies use AI for automated content creation, also known as robotic journalism.

Moreover, the field of agriculture has also witnessed the green shoots of AI and data science. Predictive analytics helps forecast crop yields, while machine learning assists in identifying plant diseases. Farmers are using drone technology combined with AI for precision farming, significantly improving productivity and sustainability.

Let's not forget about education - an area where AI is not just a tool, but a tutor. Adaptive learning systems personalize educational content for each learner, reinforcing topics where students struggle and skipping those they've mastered. Simultaneously, predictive analytics aids educational institutions in improving student outcomes by identifying those at risk of falling behind.

While these examples barely scratch the surface of how data science is revolutionizing industries, they offer a glimpse into the transformative power of AI and data science. This Section should serve as a source of inspiration and motivation for you to delve deeper and apply what you've learned in real-world contexts.

Just as we've seen the pervasive nature of data science in various sectors, remember, its true power lies in hands-on application. It's where theory meets practice, where ideas transform into tangible change. As you progress in your data science journey, continually seek ways to apply your knowledge, solve problems, and make a difference.

9 /
big data and data engineering

introduction to big data

AFTER EXPLORING the practical applications of data science, let's take a slight detour into a realm that has become an essential part of our data-driven world. Welcome to the world of big data.

Big data. It's a term you've probably heard tossed around quite a bit, but what does it really mean? Let's get a firm grasp on this concept, breaking it down into bite-sized, easily digestible pieces.

First and foremost, big data refers to incredibly large datasets that traditional data processing systems just can't handle. Whether it's the number of likes on social media platforms, financial transactions happening every nanosecond, or sensor data from millions of IoT devices, big data is all around us. It's not just about the sheer volume of data, though. Big data typically encompasses three main attributes, often referred to as the three Vs: volume, variety, and velocity.

Volume, as you might guess, refers to the massive amount of data being generated continuously. Think about how many emails you send, or how many photos you take with your smartphone. Now multiply that by billions of people doing the same thing. That's volume.

Variety speaks to the many types of data out there. We've got structured data like spreadsheets and databases, unstructured data like videos, images, and social media posts, and semi-structured data, which is a sort of mix between the two. All of these different types of data, when coming in massive volumes, contribute to the 'variety' in big data.

Velocity represents the speed at which new data is generated and the rate at which it moves around. In today's fast-paced digital world, data is being created quicker than you can blink. From real-time stock prices to live weather updates, high velocity data streams are a crucial part of big data.

Now, you might wonder, "What's the big deal about big data?" Well, the value of big data comes from the insights it can provide. When appropriately collected, analyzed, and interpreted, big data can help businesses make better decisions, scientists uncover new findings, and even governments improve their services.

However, working with big data is not without its challenges. Given its size and complexity, big data requires specific tools and techniques for storage, processing, and analysis. This is where technologies like Hadoop, Spark, and NoSQL databases come into play. These tools are designed to handle the complexities of big data, allowing us to store, process, and extract value from our massive datasets.

Privacy and security are other crucial aspects to consider when dealing with big data. Since big data often involves collecting and analyzing personal information, it's essential to handle this data responsibly and in compliance with legal and ethical standards. Cybersecurity measures are also vital to protect this data from potential threats.

Despite these challenges, the potential benefits of big data make it a cornerstone of modern data science. It allows businesses to gain a deeper understanding of their customers, helps healthcare professionals predict disease outbreaks, empowers governments to provide better services, and even aids in combating crime and fraud.

All in all, big data represents a significant aspect of our data-driven world. Its sheer size, complexity, and potential for insight are transforming the way we make decisions and understand the world around us. As budding data scientists, it's essential to grasp the concept of big data, along with the tools and techniques used to harness its power.

tools for big data: hadoop and spark

After our excursion into the realm of big data, it's time to get our hands on the tools that make handling this vast landscape possible. Let's roll up our sleeves and dive into two of the most popular big data tools – Hadoop and Spark.

Imagine you're handed a huge puzzle with billions of pieces. Trying to assemble this on your own would be an insurmountable task. But what if you could distribute the pieces among a group of friends, each working on a different part of the puzzle, and then bring everything together? Suddenly, that massive puzzle doesn't seem quite so intimidating. This is, in a nutshell, the principle behind Hadoop.

Apache Hadoop, often simply referred to as Hadoop, is an open-source software framework designed to process and store big data across clusters of computers. It's based on the MapReduce programming model, where the 'map' phase sorts and filters the data, and the 'reduce' phase summarizes it. Think of it as breaking down our puzzle into manageable chunks.

Hadoop's magic lies in its distributed processing. Data is broken up and stored across multiple nodes, and computation is carried out where the data resides. This avoids the time-consuming task of moving large volumes of data over the network. Essentially, Hadoop brings the computation to the data, not the other way around.

Two key components make up the Hadoop framework: the Hadoop Distributed File System (HDFS) and the MapReduce processing engine. HDFS provides high-throughput access to application data and is designed to span large clusters of commodity servers, while the MapReduce engine enables processing on this distributed data.

Now, let's move on to the flashier, younger sibling of Hadoop – Apache Spark. Spark is often lauded as the faster and more advanced big data tool. Like Hadoop, it can process and analyze vast datasets across a distributed computing environment. However, Spark's key selling point is speed.

Spark accomplishes its impressive speeds through in-memory processing, meaning it stores data in the RAM of servers, allowing for faster access and analysis. In contrast, Hadoop reads and writes from disk, which can be slower. That's not to say Spark replaces Hadoop. In fact, they often work together, with Spark running on top of Hadoop, leveraging HDFS for data storage.

Aside from its speed, Spark also shines with its flexibility. It comes with built-in modules for SQL, streaming, machine learning, and graph processing, making it a versatile tool for a variety of big data applications.

However, both tools come with their own sets of pros and cons. Hadoop's disk-based storage is more cost-efficient for storing massive datasets, and its robust ecosystem and wide community support can't be overlooked. On the other hand, Spark's in-memory processing makes it ideal for applications requiring real-time analytics, machine learning, or iterative algorithms.

When it comes to choosing between the two, it largely depends on your specific needs and constraints. If you're dealing with petabytes of data and budget is a concern, Hadoop's cost-efficient storage might be the way to go. However, if speed and advanced analytics are a priority, Spark could be your tool of choice.

Navigating the world of big data can seem a bit overwhelming, much like our hypothetical puzzle. But just as we would tackle the puzzle piece by piece, we approach big data bit by bit, using the right tools for the task at hand.

role of a data engineer in a data science team

Today, let's take a closer look at an integral part of any data science team - the data engineer. Now, you might be thinking, "Wait a minute, I thought we were focused on data science!" While that's true, data engineering is an often-overlooked, but incredibly crucial part of the data science process.

You can think of a data engineer as the master architect and builder who creates the solid foundation upon which the data science team constructs their analytical masterpieces. Without the meticulous work of data engineers, data scientists would find themselves knee-deep in data messes that are difficult to navigate and analyze.

So, what exactly does a data engineer do? In simple terms, a data engineer creates and maintains the systems that allow data to flow. They're responsible for creating the pipelines (aptly named "data pipelines") that bring data from various sources into a form where it can be analyzed.

Imagine that you're trying to fill a pool, but you only have a collection of small water bottles. Trying to fill the pool by emptying each water bottle one by one would be a painstakingly slow process. Instead, imagine if you could design a system of pipes that would bring the water directly from a nearby lake into the pool. That's what a data engineer does with data.

A data engineer designs, builds, and maintains the data architecture, databases, and processing systems which include the back-end data analytics systems and the data pipelines. They extract data from multiple sources, transform it (often cleaning and enriching the data), and load it into these systems, a process known as ETL (Extract, Transform, Load). They ensure that large volumes of data are processed and prepared for analysis in an efficient, timely, and accurate manner.

But a data engineer's role doesn't stop there. They also ensure that these systems are reliable, scalable, and robust, able to handle the ever-increasing volumes of data that modern businesses deal with. This requires in-depth knowledge of big data technologies and tools like Hadoop, Spark, and NoSQL databases, along with strong software engineering skills to build custom solutions as needed.

Data engineers also take the lead in ensuring that data is accessible and secure. They need to design systems that allow easy access to data for analysis while also ensuring that sensitive information is protected, meeting all data governance and compliance standards.

In a data science team, the data engineer's work forms the basis for all further analysis. After all, if the data isn't correctly collected, stored, and prepared, the insights derived from it are likely to be flawed or misleading. Their work supports not only data scientists but also data analysts and business intelligence professionals, providing them with the data they need for their work.

In essence, data engineers are a bit like the unsung heroes of data science. While they might not be in the spotlight as often as data scientists, their work plays a crucial role in enabling effective data analysis. They keep the data flowing smoothly, ensuring that everyone on the team can do their job to the best of their abilities.

10 /
time series and
forecasting

understanding time series data

TODAY, we're going to delve into the world of time series data - a critical type of data that shows up in so many places, from stock market trends to weather patterns, and from heart rate readings to website traffic.

Time series data, as the name implies, is a series of data points listed in time order. It's like a diary that nature, humans, or machines keep, logging what happens at each moment in time. Every entry in this diary is time-stamped, meaning it's associated with a particular point in time. This temporal order is what distinguishes time series data from other types of data, making it uniquely challenging and fascinating to analyze.

To illustrate, let's think about a retail store that records its sales every day. Each day, the store logs how many items were sold. This set of daily sales figures forms a time series. With this time series data, the store can observe patterns and trends over time, identify busy and slow periods, and make data-driven decisions to boost sales.

One important aspect of time series data is that it's sequential. The order of data points matters, and the correlation between one point and the points before and after it is often significant. This characteristic makes time series data fundamentally different from cross-sectional data, where each data point is independent.

In the world of data science, time series analysis is a whole field in itself. It involves various techniques for analyzing time series data to extract meaningful statistics and other characteristics. It's about understanding the past, analyzing the present, and predicting the future.

For example, consider a time series of daily temperatures in a city. Time series analysis could help us identify whether there's a warming or cooling trend over the years. Or we could spot patterns within a year, like identifying which months tend to be the hottest or coldest. We could also use it to predict future temperatures.

Two essential concepts in time series analysis are 'trend' and 'seasonality'. A trend is a long-term increase or decrease in the data. It doesn't have to be linear, and sometimes we might see a series of rises and falls that still suggest a general direction. Seasonality, on the other hand, is a pattern that repeats at regular intervals, like the changing of seasons or the cycle of day and night.

But the magic of time series analysis doesn't stop there. It can also help us detect anomalies - points in time where data behaves unusually. Spotting these can be crucial in various contexts, from detecting fraud in financial transactions to identifying system faults in machine logs.

Now, you may wonder, how do we deal with time series data in practice? Python, the Swiss army knife of data science, comes to the rescue once again. Libraries like Pandas make handling time series data easier, and libraries like statsmodels and Prophet help with the analysis part.

However, time series analysis does have its challenges. It often involves dealing with noise and uncertainty. The data may also have missing points, or the pattern may change over time, a phenomenon known as concept drift.

But despite these challenges, the rewards of understanding time series data are immense. It's a type of data that encodes the story of how things evolve and change. By learning to analyze it, we can become better at understanding the world, making predictions, and informing our decisions with data.

techniques for time series forecasting

In our last Section, we traveled through the fascinating world of time series data, understanding its significance and challenges. Today, we're going to delve deeper into the treasure chest of time series analysis and discuss time series forecasting techniques. These methods are powerful tools in your data science arsenal, enabling you to make future predictions based on past data. Let's dive right in!

Forecasting is a crucial component of decision-making in a wide variety of fields. Economists forecast market trends, meteorologists predict weather patterns, businesses project sales and revenue - the list is endless. In the heart of all these activities, we often find time series data and the powerful forecasting methods that transform historical information into future insights.

The first technique we'll discuss is moving averages. In a nutshell, a moving average forecast uses the average of the most recent data points to predict the next one. It's simple but effective when your time series data is relatively stable and doesn't show strong trends or seasonal patterns.

Next in line is the method of exponential smoothing. This technique still averages recent data points, but it assigns them with exponentially decreasing weights as they get older. The advantage here is that it provides a way to "forget" older data gradually, making the model more responsive to recent changes.

However, if your data exhibit a trend or seasonality, you might need a more sophisticated method, like the Holt-Winters method. This technique extends exponential smoothing to capture these additional patterns in the data.

Now, if we have to bring out the big guns for forecasting, we're talking about ARIMA - AutoRegressive Integrated Moving Average. This method is a combination of autoregression (modeling the next step in the sequence as a linear function of the observations at prior time steps), differencing (to remove trend and seasonality), and moving average model. It's a flexible and robust approach, but it requires a good understanding of your data and careful tuning.

As we delve into more modern methods, we meet the prophet, a forecasting tool developed by Facebook. The Prophet is designed to handle the common features of business time series, such as trends, seasonality, and holidays, making it a powerful tool for various real-world forecasting tasks.

But time series forecasting isn't limited to traditional statistical methods. Machine learning, too, has a role to play. Regression models can be adapted to time series forecasting tasks, as can more advanced techniques like support vector machines and random forests.

In the realm of deep learning, we have Recurrent Neural Networks (RNNs), which are designed explicitly for handling sequential data. And one particularly powerful type of RNN is the Long Short-Term Memory (LSTM) network. LSTM networks can learn long-term dependencies, making them highly effective for many time series forecasting problems.

The choice of forecasting technique often depends on the specifics of your data and the nature of your forecasting task. One size doesn't fit all. Remember, it's always important to understand your data first, and then choose and tune your model accordingly.

It's worth mentioning that all these methods, from moving averages to LSTM networks, are available in Python. Libraries like statsmodels, scikit-learn, and Keras provide comprehensive tools to handle these tasks.

In essence, time series forecasting is a journey from understanding the past to predicting the future. And while the path can be winding and full of challenges, the view from the end is truly worth it. The ability to peek into the future, even if imperfectly, is a powerful tool that can inform decision-making in countless ways.

hands-on: time series analysis using python

Previously, we've navigated the theory behind time series forecasting. Now, it's time to roll up our sleeves, dive into some Python code, and see these concepts in action. After all, data science isn't just about understanding; it's about doing. Ready? Let's get started!

To get started with time series analysis in Python, we first need to import a few libraries. We'll need pandas for data handling, numpy for numerical operations, matplotlib and seaborn for data visualization, and finally, statsmodels for the time series analysis itself. Let's import these:

```python
import pandas as pd
import numpy as np
import matplotlib.pyplot as plt
import seaborn as sns
from statsmodels.tsa.arima_model import ARIMA
```

from statsmodels.tsa.seasonal import seasonal_decompose
```

Alright, let's load some time series data. For this walkthrough, we'll use the popular "AirPassengers" dataset, which contains the total number of airline passengers for each month from 1949 to 1960.
```python
df = pd.read_csv('AirPassengers.csv', parse_dates = ['Month'], index_col = ['Month'])
```

We use `parse_dates` to tell pandas to interpret the 'Month' column as dates, and `index_col` to use 'Month' as the index of our dataframe, which is necessary for time series analysis.

With the data loaded, let's take a quick peek using the `head()` function:
```python
print(df.head())
```

Okay, now let's visualize our data using matplotlib:
```python
plt.figure(figsize=(10,6))
plt.plot(df.index, df['#Passengers'], '--', marker='*',)
plt.grid()
plt.xlabel('Year')
plt.title('Airline Passengers from 1949 to 1960')
```
```

```python
plt.show()
```

Now we have a nice plot showing the trend and seasonality in our data.

Next, let's decompose our time series to observe the trend, seasonality, and residuals more clearly. We can use the `seasonal_decompose` function from the `statsmodels` library for this.

```python
decomposition = seasonal_decompose(df['#Passengers'])
trend = decomposition.trend
seasonal = decomposition.seasonal
residual = decomposition.resid
plt.figure(figsize=(12,8))
plt.subplot(411)
plt.plot(df['#Passengers'], label='Original')
plt.subplot(412)
plt.plot(trend, label='Trend')
plt.subplot(413)
plt.plot(seasonal,label='Seasonality')
plt.subplot(414)
plt.plot(residual, label='Residuals')
plt.tight_layout()
plt.show()
```

Now, let's dive into forecasting. We'll use the

ARIMA model, one of the most common methods for time series forecasting.

First, we need to find the optimal parameters for our ARIMA model. This involves selecting the best values for `p`, `d`, and `q`, which represent the order of the autoregressive, differencing, and moving average parts of the model, respectively. This is often done using the Autocorrelation and Partial Autocorrelation plots, but for simplicity, we'll use (2,1,0) as our parameters.

```python
model = ARIMA(df['#Passengers'], order=(2,1,0))
model_fit = model.fit(disp=0)
```

With our model fitted, we can make forecasts. Here, we'll forecast the next 2 years, or 24 steps ahead.

```python
forecast = model_fit.forecast(steps = 24)
```

Now we can plot the forecasted data alongside the original data:

```python
plt.figure(figsize=(10,6))
plt.plot(df.index, df['#Passengers'], '--', marker='*',)
plt.plot(pd.date_range(df.index[-1], periods = 24, freq='M'), forecast[0], color = 'red')
plt.grid()
```

```
plt.xlabel('Year')
plt.title('Airline Passengers from 1949 to 1960 with Forecast')
plt.show()
```

And there we have it! We've performed time series analysis and forecasting on the AirPassengers dataset using Python.

One thing to remember is that time series analysis can be a complex process. There are many factors to consider and many decisions to make along the way. While we used the ARIMA model here, there are many other models and techniques to consider depending on the specific characteristics of your time series data.

11 /
recommender systems

the theory behind recommender systems

WE'RE NOW TURNING our attention to a fascinating, and often underestimated, piece of the data science puzzle - recommender systems. What's the first thing you think about when I mention recommender systems? Netflix movie suggestions? Amazon product recommendations? Or perhaps it's Spotify's uncanny ability to suggest that song you didn't know you needed? These systems have become integral parts of our digital lives, subtly guiding us through a world of overwhelming choices. But what's the magic behind them? Let's unravel this mystery together.

Recommender systems are data filtering tools that use algorithms to predict a user's preference or interest towards a particular item or product. They're key elements in modern e-commerce and media platforms, assisting in the delivery of personalized content and offers to users. By creating an individualized experience, recommender systems not only enhance user satisfaction but also drive additional sales and user engagement for businesses.

But how do these systems make such accurate predictions? It's not magic, my friend, but a beautiful interplay of mathematics and computer science. To understand this, we need to delve into the two primary types of recommender systems: Collaborative Filtering (CF) and Content-Based Filtering (CB).

Collaborative Filtering is a method that analyzes the interactions between users and items. It's like asking for a book recommendation from a friend who has similar taste. The main assumption here is that users who agreed in the past will agree again in the future. CF can be user-based, where recommendations are based on users similar to you, or item-based, where recommendations are based on items similar to those you liked.

User-based CF operates on the principle that if two users agree on one issue, they are likely to agree again in the future. Essentially, if User A and User B both liked the same books, and User B enjoyed another book that User A hasn't read yet, the system will recommend that book to User A. It's like when a friend who shares your taste in movies recommends a film they just saw and loved.

In contrast, item-based CF focuses on the relationships between items. It's all about understanding patterns in user behavior to find similarities between different items. If users who bought a certain type of running shoes also tend to buy a specific brand of running socks, the system will start recommending those socks to other users who bought the same shoes.

Now, let's turn our attention to Content-Based Filtering. This method relies more on the properties of items rather than user-item interactions. It's like asking a librarian for a book recommendation based on the fact you like fantasy novels. The system would then suggest other fantasy books for you to read.

Content-Based Filtering involves creating a profile for each item by representing it as a set of descriptors, such as the words in a document, the genre of a movie, or the category of a product. It then matches these item profiles to a user's profile, which is made up of their preferences and past behavior, to recommend items that most closely align with the user's profile.

Of course, there's a third type of recommender system that combines both approaches, appropriately called Hybrid Recommender Systems. They aim to leverage the strengths of both CF and CB while compensating for their weaknesses. For instance, Netflix uses a hybrid model incorporating both collaborative and content-based filtering in its recommendation engine.

The magic of recommender systems isn't about pulling a rabbit out of a hat. It's in the fascinating world of patterns, similarities, and data that surrounds us. From user-user similarities to user-item interactions, these systems weave a complex tapestry that subtly guides us through our digital journeys. And though they might seem complex at first glance, I hope our discussion today has shed some light on how they work behind the scenes.

building a basic recommender system

In our previous Section, we delved into the fascinating world of recommender systems, exploring their underlying concepts and techniques. Now, it's time to roll up our sleeves and put theory into practice. Yes, you guessed it! Today, we're going to build our very own basic recommender system. It's an exciting milestone on our data science journey, and I'm thrilled to be your guide.

Before we set sail, let's make sure we have all the necessary tools. To build our recommender system, we'll be using Python, a powerful and versatile programming language that's a favorite among data scientists. We'll also be leveraging the power of pandas, a popular data manipulation library, and scikit-learn, a comprehensive machine learning library. If you haven't installed these libraries already, you can do so using pip, Python's package manager.

First, let's start with the basics. What does a recommender system need? At the core, it needs data, specifically user-item interactions. For our journey, we'll use a simple dataset containing movie ratings from users. You can download this dataset from the MovieLens website or use any other dataset that consists of user-item interactions.

Let's load our data using pandas and take a peek:

```python
import pandas as pd
ratings = pd.read_csv('ratings.csv')
print(ratings.head())
```

Once our data is loaded, the next step is to calculate the average rating for each movie. This will give us a general idea of the overall reception of the movies.

```python
average_ratings = ratings.groupby('movieId')['rating'].mean()
print(average_ratings.head())
```

Our next step involves calculating the number of ratings each movie has received. This is an important step because the average rating alone can be misleading. A movie with an average rating of 5 stars isn't impressive if it has only been rated by one person!

```python
count_ratings = ratings.groupby('movieId')['rating'].count()
print(count_ratings.head())
```

Now that we have the average ratings and the number of ratings, let's create a new DataFrame to hold these values:

```python
ratings_stats = pd.DataFrame({
'AverageRating': average_ratings,
'NumberOfRatings': count_ratings
})
print(ratings_stats.head())
```

So far, we've created a simple system that recommends the highest-rated movies. But let's make it a bit more nuanced by considering both the average rating and the number of ratings. We'll define a weighted rating, which gives more importance to movies with more ratings.

```python
```

```python
v = ratings_stats['NumberOfRatings']
R = ratings_stats['AverageRating']
C = ratings_stats['AverageRating'].mean()
m = ratings_stats['NumberOfRatings'].quantile(0.70)
ratings_stats['WeightedRating'] = (v / (v + m) * R) + (m / (m + v) * C)
```

Finally, we sort our DataFrame based on the weighted rating and voila, we have a basic recommender system!

```python
recommended_movies = ratings_stats.sort_values('WeightedRating', ascending=False)
print(recommended_movies.head())
```

Phew! That was a journey, wasn't it? Together, we've taken a theoretical concept and turned it into a tangible piece of code. It's like taking a recipe and turning it into a delicious dish.

While this recommender system is pretty basic, it serves as a solid foundation. As we progress, we can incorporate more complex techniques and fine-tune our system to cater to different tastes and preferences.

advanced recommender systems: collaborative filtering and deep learning

After our hands-on experience building a basic recommender system, we're all set to go beyond and explore the intricacies of more advanced recommender systems. In this Section, we're going to tackle two power-packed concepts: Collaborative Filtering and Deep Learning. Ready to dive in? Great, let's get started!

To recall, a recommender system is a sophisticated tool that filters information to predict what a user may or may not like. Now, among the multiple techniques to build these systems, Collaborative Filtering (CF) is one of the most popular ones. In a nutshell, CF predicts a user's interests by collecting preferences from many users. Think of it as asking your friends for movie recommendations, but on a much, much larger scale.

CF can be further divided into two types: User-based and Item-based. User-based CF recommends items by finding users who are similar to the targeted user. Think of it as saying, "People who are similar to you also liked these items, so you might too!" On the other hand, Item-based CF recommends items that are similar to items the user has already liked. This is akin to saying, "Since you liked this item, you might also like these similar ones."

Let's move on to our next topic: Deep Learning. We've all heard of this buzzword, haven't we? In simple terms, Deep Learning is a subset of machine learning where neural networks learn from vast amounts of data. Deep Learning can power recommender systems to capture more complex patterns and make more accurate recommendations.

Now, let's see how we can use these techniques in our recommender system.

First, let's look at implementing CF using the Surprise library in Python:

```python
from surprise import KNNBasic
from surprise import Dataset
from surprise import Reader
from surprise.model_selection import cross_validate
# Load the data
reader = Reader(rating_scale=(1, 5))
data = Dataset.load_from_df(ratings[['userId', 'movieId', 'rating']], reader)
# Use user-based collaborative filtering
algo = KNNBasic(sim_options={'user_based': True})
# Run 5-fold cross-validation and print results
```

```
cross_validate(algo, data, measures=['RMSE',
'MAE'], cv=5, verbose=True)
```

For deep learning, we can use the powerful Keras library to create a simple deep learning model. Note that this requires more computational power and may take some time to run:

```python
from keras.layers import Input, Embedding, Flatten, Dot, Dense
from keras.models import Model
# Creating the model
movie_input = Input(shape=[1], name="Movie-Input")
movie_embedding = Embedding(num_movies+1, 5, name="Movie-Embedding")(movie_input)
movie_vec = Flatten(name="Flatten-Movies")(movie_embedding)
user_input = Input(shape=[1], name="User-Input")
user_embedding = Embedding(num_users+1, 5, name="User-Embedding")(user_input)
user_vec = Flatten(name="Flatten-Users")(user_embedding)
prod = Dot(name="Dot-Product", axes=1)([movie_vec, user_vec])
model = Model([user_input, movie_input], prod)
model.compile('adam', 'mean_squared_error')
```

```
# Training the model
model.fit([train.userId, train.movieId], train.rating,
epochs=10, verbose=1)
```

Note that `num_users` and `num_movies` are the total number of unique users and movies in your dataset, respectively.

By now, you should have a fair understanding of how to leverage the power of collaborative filtering and deep learning for building more advanced recommender systems. However, these methods are just the tip of the iceberg. The field of recommender systems is continually evolving, with new techniques and methods coming up regularly. So, keep exploring and keep experimenting.

12 /
building a data science portfolio

importance of a portfolio for data scientists

THE JOURNEY we've been on together has covered a lot of fascinating territory, hasn't it? From understanding the nitty-gritty of machine learning algorithms to exploring the potential of neural networks, we've delved into the world of data science, savoring its many flavors. Today, we're going to discuss a critical aspect that often goes unmentioned in technical textbooks: the importance of a portfolio for data scientists.

In our hyper-connected world, where data is abundant and opportunities aplenty, standing out from the crowd is crucial. The same is true in the field of data science. You might have a profound understanding of theories, and your programming skills may be top-notch, but how do you showcase this to potential employers or collaborators? This is where a portfolio comes into play. Think of it as your personalized showcase, a tangible demonstration of your skills, competencies, and what you can bring to the table.

Now, you might be wondering, what should a data science portfolio include? In essence, it should be a representation of you as a professional. It should include your completed projects, highlighting the problems you've tackled, the datasets you've wrangled, and the insights you've unearthed. Whether it's a machine learning model you've built from scratch, an exploratory data analysis project, or an end-to-end data pipeline you've constructed, each piece is a testament to your capabilities.

Remember that your portfolio is not just about the final product; it's also about the journey. Document your thought process, the steps you took, the methods you used, the challenges you faced, and how you overcame them. This will provide viewers with a window into how you approach problems and will give them confidence in your problem-solving abilities.

Let's delve deeper into what makes a compelling data science portfolio.

First and foremost, diversity is key. A portfolio that showcases a broad range of skills—data cleaning, visualization, statistical analysis, machine learning—is more likely to impress. This tells your potential employer that you can wear many hats and that you're not a one-trick pony.

Secondly, don't shy away from showing off your coding skills. Providing well-documented code on platforms like GitHub not only demonstrates your technical proficiency but also exhibits your ability to work in a collaborative environment, an essential trait for modern data science teams.

A third crucial aspect is storytelling. Data science is not just about number crunching; it's about telling a story with the data. Thus, projects that clearly articulate the problem, the approach, and the solution in an engaging and accessible manner will set you apart.

Finally, a significant portion of data science work involves domain knowledge. Projects that demonstrate your ability to understand, interpret, and apply domain knowledge—be it in healthcare, finance, marketing, or any other sector—will highlight your versatility.

Now, with a clearer understanding of what makes a strong portfolio, let's talk about how to build one. If you're just starting, choose a few datasets you find interesting and start exploring. Websites like Kaggle, UCI Machine Learning Repository, and Google's Dataset Search are excellent starting points. As you become more comfortable, move on to more complex projects, such as predictive modeling or building machine learning algorithms.

Remember that your portfolio is a living document. It should grow and evolve as you do professionally. Keep updating it with new projects, learnings, and skills. Also, don't forget to include feedback loops in your portfolio—provide ways for people to reach out and connect with you, be it through email, LinkedIn, or GitHub.

While building a robust data science portfolio takes time and effort, the payoff is worth it. Not only does it make you more visible to potential employers, but it also aids your learning process. Each project you add to your portfolio solidifies your understanding and hones your problem-solving skills.

projects to demonstrate your skills

It's always a pleasure to guide you further into the world of data science. Just imagine - with every concept you learn and every skill you master, you're becoming an even more impressive force in this field. And there's no better way to demonstrate your expertise than with a well-crafted project. In this Section, we will discuss a variety of projects you can undertake to showcase your skills.

Before we dive in, let's start with some general

advice: Pick projects that genuinely interest you. This not only keeps the process enjoyable but also fuels your curiosity and drives you to dig deeper, ask better questions, and uncover more intriguing insights.

Alright, now let's get down to business and talk about some potential projects you might consider.

1. Predictive Modelling: This is an excellent starting point for demonstrating your grasp of machine learning concepts. You might choose to predict housing prices, for example, based on a variety of features like location, square footage, number of bedrooms, and so on. Or perhaps you want to forecast stock prices or predict whether a customer will churn. This type of project showcases your ability to prepare data, select an appropriate model, train it, and make predictions.

2. Text Mining and Natural Language Processing (NLP): Do you want to showcase your NLP skills? Consider a sentiment analysis project where you analyze social media posts or product reviews to determine whether the overall sentiment is positive, negative, or neutral. Alternatively, you could create a chatbot, which would show your ability to process and generate natural language responses.

3. Image Classification: If you're interested in computer vision, consider a project that involves classifying images. This could be something like a facial recognition system or a model that classifies different

types of animals or vehicles. Such a project would demonstrate your understanding of Convolutional Neural Networks (CNNs).

4. Time Series Analysis: Do you want to forecast the future? A time series analysis project might be right up your alley. This could involve predicting future sales for a company, forecasting weather patterns, or estimating stock prices. Such a project emphasizes your understanding of trends, seasonality, and autocorrelation.

5. Anomaly Detection: You could work on a project that identifies fraudulent credit card transactions or flags unusual activity in network traffic. An anomaly detection project like this illustrates your ability to handle imbalanced datasets and your understanding of algorithms designed for this kind of task.

6. Recommendation Systems: Building a recommendation engine, such as those used by Netflix or Amazon, is another project option. This demonstrates your understanding of collaborative filtering, content-based filtering, and perhaps even some deep learning.

Remember that it's not just about completing the project but also about showcasing your work effectively. Document your process and your findings clearly. Include visualizations that help tell the story of your data. And don't forget to discuss the challenges you encountered and how you overcame them.

how to showcase your work online

Welcome back, future data science gurus! You've made it this far, and I bet you're brimming with new knowledge and skills. Now, it's time to take all that hard work and present it to the world. In this Section, we'll discuss how to showcase your work online effectively.

Creating a portfolio and showcasing your work online is like preparing a visually appealing, interactive resume. It's your opportunity to grab attention, make a strong impression, and demonstrate your understanding of data science concepts. But, how do you go about doing this? Let's dig into that.

1. Select the Right Projects: Start by choosing a few projects that you're proud of and that best represent your skills. These could be projects from a range of areas, including predictive modelling, text mining, image classification, or time series analysis. Diversification is key here; it shows that you're adaptable and capable of tackling various problems.

2. Document Your Process: Make sure you document every step of your project. Include the problem you were addressing, the data you used, your approach, any challenges you encountered, and, of course, your results. It's not just about the outcome; employers want to see how you think and how you approach problems.

3. Use Visuals: Graphs, charts, and other visuals aren't just appealing; they can make complex data much easier to understand. Be sure to include clear, easy-to-read visualizations that complement your written content.

4. Clean, Commented Code: Your code is a testament to your technical ability. Make sure it's not just functional but also neat and well-organized. Include comments explaining what each block of code does. This makes it easier for anyone (including future you) to understand your logic.

5. Make It Interactive: If possible, make your portfolio interactive. This could mean including code that can be run directly on the site or creating interactive visuals using tools like D3.js or Tableau.

6. Use the Right Platform: Platforms like GitHub and Kaggle are popular places to share data science projects. They allow you to share your code and provide tools for visualization. You might also consider creating a personal website or blog where you can share your projects, along with articles or tutorials on topics you're passionate about.

7. Share Your Work: Once your work is online, don't be shy about sharing it. Post it on LinkedIn, share it on Twitter, or include it in online data science communities. You never know who might see it and what opportunities it could lead to.

Remember, the goal of showcasing your work online is to tell a story about who you are as a data scientist. It's about more than just the technical details; it's about your approach to problem-solving, your creativity, your grit in the face of challenging problems, and your ability to communicate complex ideas in an accessible way.

preparing for data science interviews

typical data science interview questions

NOW THAT YOU'VE amassed a wide array of data science skills, built a stellar portfolio, and learned how to showcase it to the world, you're undoubtedly ready to take on the job market. But before you start sending out applications, let's prepare for an essential step of the process: the interview. In this Section, we'll go through some typical data science interview questions and how best to approach them.

The data science interview is a test of your skills, knowledge, and personality. It's designed to assess not only what you know but also how you solve problems, how you communicate, and whether you'd be a good fit for the team and the organization.

1. Technical Questions

You're sure to face technical questions in a data science interview. Here, the interviewer wants to see your understanding and application of data science concepts. Let's start with a few examples:

- *What is the Central Limit Theorem and why is it important?*

This question is about your understanding of fundamental statistics. In answering this, you'll want to discuss the theorem, its assumptions, and its implications, especially its significance in hypothesis testing and the creation of confidence intervals.

- *What are the differences between supervised and unsupervised learning?*

Here, you'll want to define both, discuss the key differences, and provide examples of algorithms and practical applications for each.

. . .

- *Can you explain how a random forest model works?*

This question tests your knowledge of specific machine learning algorithms. You'll want to describe the algorithm's fundamental components, its workings, and its benefits and drawbacks.

2. Coding Questions

Expect to tackle some coding challenges during your interview. The interviewer wants to verify your coding skills and your familiarity with algorithms and data structures. You might be asked something like:

- *Write a function to find the second largest number in an array.*
Here, you'll need to demonstrate your command of the language and your ability to write efficient, clean code.

3. Problem-Solving Questions

. . .

These questions assess your analytical skills and your ability to apply data science methods to solve real-world problems. For example:

- *How would you predict customer churn?*
    This question is looking for a step-by-step explanation of how you'd approach this problem, including the kind of data you'd need, the exploratory data analysis steps you'd take, and the models you might use.

4. Behavioral Questions

Finally, expect some behavioral questions. These are meant to assess how you'd fit into the team and the company culture. For example:

- *Tell me about a time when you had to deal with a difficult team member.*
    With such questions, be honest but positive. Discuss how you handled the situation and what you learned from it.

. . .

Remember, there are no "perfect" answers to these questions. What matters is that you can demonstrate a strong understanding of data science fundamentals, apply that understanding to solve problems, and communicate your thought process clearly and effectively.

Interviews can be daunting, but remember, they're also an opportunity. They allow you to learn more about the company, the team, and the kinds of problems they're facing. So go in with confidence, curiosity, and an eagerness to share your passion for data science.

preparing for technical interviews

You've made great progress on your data science journey, and you're now ready to face one of the final hurdles: technical interviews. These types of interviews may seem intimidating at first, but with proper preparation, you can approach them with confidence and poise. In this Section, we're going to tackle the ins and outs of preparing for technical interviews.

. . .

1. Know What to Expect

Technical interviews are a common part of the hiring process in the data science world. These interviews typically involve solving real-world problems and coding challenges that test your knowledge of algorithms, data structures, and language syntax.

Remember, the interviewer isn't just evaluating your ability to solve the problem but also observing your problem-solving process. Can you think analytically? Can you adapt when you hit a roadblock? Are you able to clearly and concisely explain your thought process?

2. Brush Up on Your Theory

Start your preparations by reviewing the core concepts and theories of data science. The topics might range from statistics and probability, machine learning algorithms, data wrangling, to data visualization. While you won't be expected to recite definitions verbatim, you should be comfortable explaining these concepts and discussing how they're applied in a data science context.

3. Practice Coding

In a data science technical interview, you'll likely face coding challenges. Spend time coding every day. Use platforms like LeetCode, HackerRank, and Kaggle to practice. These platforms have problems ranging from easy to hard, allowing you to gradually level up your skills.

Focus on Python or R, as they are the most common languages in data science. You should also familiarize yourself with SQL, as it's often used for data retrieval in data science.

4. Review Data Structures and Algorithms

While you may not need to implement a binary search tree or perform a quicksort from scratch, under-standing common data structures and algorithms is crucial. This knowledge will help you write more efficient code and better solve the problems presented in technical interviews.

5. Work on Mock Interviews and Whiteboarding

Whiteboarding refers to solving problems on a whiteboard (or similar medium) while explaining your thought process. It can feel unnatural, especially if you're used to coding on your computer. Practicing this can make a significant difference.

Mock interviews can also be incredibly helpful. Team up with a fellow data science aspirant and take turns interviewing each other. There are also platforms online that offer mock interview services.

6. Know the Company and Role

Before your interview, research the company and the specific role for which you're applying. Understanding the company's products, culture, and values can help you tailor your responses to show why you're a great fit.

7. Stay Healthy and Rested

Finally, make sure to take care of your physical health leading up to your interviews. Get plenty of rest, eat healthily, and take breaks during your preparation. This will help ensure that you're at your best on the day of the interview.

Technical interviews might seem like a steep mountain to climb. However, with adequate preparation, you can transform this challenge into a stepping stone towards your dream data science job. Take it one step at a time, and remember, the goal is progress, not perfection.

tips and tricks for acing your interviews

You've gained considerable knowledge throughout this journey, and now, it's time to take a step further and dive into some practical tips and tricks to help you excel in your upcoming interviews. After all, interviews are your chance to demonstrate your skills, experience, and personality to your potential employers. Let's get right into it!

1. Know Your Resume Inside Out

Your resume is more than just a document; it's a story of your professional journey. Each project, each role, and each skill you've included speaks to your abilities and experiences. Be ready to discuss anything listed on your resume in detail, providing concrete examples of your achievements and the impact you made.

2. Communicate Your Thought Process Clearly

During the technical portion of the interview, your thought process can be just as important as the final answer. Be sure to articulate your thoughts clearly and systematically. Show them how you approach problems, how you deal with challenges, and how you iterate on solutions. This provides insight into your problem-solving skills and your potential as a team member.

. . .

3. Highlight Your Projects

Projects are a tangible demonstration of your skills and expertise. When discussing your projects, talk about the problem you addressed, how you approached it, what tools and techniques you used, the challenges you faced, and how you overcame them. Don't forget to mention the impact and results of your work.

4. Showcase Your Knowledge in Data Science

Your depth of knowledge in data science will be under the spotlight during interviews. Be prepared to discuss a wide range of topics, from statistical concepts, machine learning algorithms, and data structures, to coding, data cleaning, and visualization techniques. Stay updated with the latest trends and advancements in the field too!

5. Explain Complex Concepts Simply

. . .

As a data scientist, you'll often need to explain complex data science concepts to stakeholders with non-technical backgrounds. Demonstrate this ability in your interviews. If you're asked about a complex concept or technique, try to explain it in a way that someone without a data science background could understand.

6. Be Curious and Ask Questions

Remember, an interview is a two-way conversation. Asking thoughtful questions shows your interest in the role and the company. You might ask about the company culture, the team you'll be working with, the projects you'll initially work on, or how the company uses data science in its operations.

7. Brush Up on Relevant Tools and Languages

Whether it's Python, R, SQL, or specific libraries and frameworks like pandas, scikit-learn, TensorFlow, or PyTorch, make sure you're comfortable with the tools mentioned in the job description. Practice using these tools in different scenarios to prepare for technical questions or coding tests.

8. Show Enthusiasm

Enthusiasm can set you apart from other candidates. Show your passion for data science and for the role you're applying for. This can be contagious and make you memorable to the interviewers.

9. Practice, Practice, Practice

Whether it's technical skills or behavioral questions, practice is key. Use online platforms to practice coding and problem-solving. Mock interviews can also be very useful.

10. Learn from Every Interview

. . .

Every interview, whether it leads to a job offer or not, is a learning opportunity. Seek feedback, reflect on your performance, and identify areas for improvement.

With these tips in your back pocket, you're well on your way to acing your data science interviews. Remember, confidence is key, and that comes from being well-prepared and understanding your value. Go in with the mindset that the interview is as much for you to understand the company as it is for the company to understand you.

14 /

continuing your
data science journey

lifelong learning in data science

WITH ALL THE knowledge we've amassed and the strategies we've discussed so far, it's time to talk about something vital that underpins the entire data science profession: lifelong learning.

In the realm of data science, the only constant is change. The field is evolving at an unparalleled pace, with new tools, techniques, algorithms, and paradigms emerging all the time. As such, a successful data scientist is defined not just by their foundational skills, but by their ability to adapt, learn, and grow over time.

1. Evolving Landscape of Data Science

The first thing to understand about lifelong learning in data science is that it's not just a nice-to-have; it's essential. The technologies, tools, and techniques that are considered cutting-edge today may be outdated in a few years, or even a few months. From new programming languages and libraries to groundbreaking machine learning models and big data technologies, the field is in constant flux. Staying abreast of these changes can help you to continue delivering high-quality, relevant work.

2. Online Learning Platforms

With the advent of online learning platforms, it's easier than ever to keep your knowledge up-to-date. Platforms like Coursera, Udemy, edX, and Khan Academy offer courses in everything from basic Python programming to advanced deep learning. Often, these courses are taught by experts from leading universities or companies, offering high-quality, current instruction.

3. Data Science Blogs and Podcasts

In addition to structured courses, blogs and podcasts can be fantastic resources for staying current in the field of data science. Some of the best learning happens informally, and these resources often provide insights into real-world applications, industry trends, and expert opinions. Some popular ones include the Towards Data Science blog, the Data Skeptic podcast, and the AI Alignment podcast.

4. Active Engagement in the Data Science Community

Participation in the data science community can greatly accelerate your learning. This might involve contributing to open-source projects, attending meetups or conferences, or participating in online forums like Stack Overflow or GitHub. These communities can be a great place to learn from others' experiences, get feedback on your work, and gain exposure to new ideas and perspectives.

5. Data Science Competitions

Platforms like Kaggle offer data science competitions that can be a fun and challenging way to test and grow your skills. These competitions can expose you to new problems and techniques, and the competition format can provide a powerful motivation to learn. Additionally, doing well in these competitions can add a valuable credential to your portfolio.

6. Research Papers and Journals

For those at the cutting edge of the field, research papers and academic journals can be a vital source of learning. Journals like the Journal of Machine Learning Research and conferences like NeurIPS are where the latest methods and discoveries are shared. Reading these papers can give you an understanding of where the field is heading.

7. Learning from Failure

Lastly, but perhaps most importantly, is learning from failure. As a data scientist, you're likely to encounter many challenges and setbacks. These are not just inevitable, but are valuable learning opportunities. By analyzing what went wrong, you can gain deep insights and improve for the future.

staying updated: blogs, podcasts, and conferences

Well, hello there, fellow data enthusiasts! If you're reading this, you've probably already embraced the mindset of lifelong learning that's so integral to our profession. But what's the secret sauce to staying current in a field as dynamic and rapidly evolving as data science? The answer is simple: immersing yourself in the world of data science through various resources like blogs, podcasts, and conferences. So, let's dive into how these can help you keep your finger on the pulse of the data science world.

1. The Power of Blogs

Blogs are a goldmine of knowledge in data science. They're the medium where professionals, hobbyists, and thought leaders share their insights, experiences, and the latest trends in the industry. From tutorial-driven blogs that help you master new skills to opinion pieces that can expand your thinking, the blogosphere is buzzing with valuable content.

One outstanding blog to bookmark is 'Towards

Data Science'. It's a Medium publication offering a mix of articles covering various data science topics. From practical tutorials to pieces exploring the theoretical underpinnings of machine learning, it has something for everyone.

KDnuggets is another go-to resource, known for its news, tutorials, and posts on a variety of data science topics. The site also conducts regular polls on data science trends, offering a fascinating snapshot of the field at any given time.

2. The Wisdom of Podcasts

If you're someone who absorbs information better through listening, podcasts are the perfect fit for you. They're a great way to turn travel or downtime into a learning opportunity.

One standout example is the 'Data Skeptic' podcast, which takes complex data science concepts and breaks them down in an accessible way. It's a balanced mix of technical detail and high-level overview, making it suitable for both beginners and experienced profes-sionals.

Then there's the 'Not So Standard Deviations' podcast. Hosted by Roger Peng and Hilary Parker, it offers an insightful and entertaining look at the world of data science, from the perspective of two industry insiders.

3. The Networking at Conferences

Conferences are a fantastic way to engage with the data science community. They offer a chance to learn from industry leaders, share your ideas, and even meet potential employers or collaborators. Plus, many conferences also offer hands-on workshops where you can boost your practical skills.

The Neural Information Processing Systems conference (NeurIPS) is a must-attend event if you're into machine learning and computational neuroscience. It's where the most recent breakthroughs are discussed and future trends predicted.

On the big data front, the Strata Data Conference is a heavy hitter. It brings together data scientists, analysts, and executives from a variety of industries to share insights, challenges, and best practices in handling big data.

4. Other Avenues to Explore

Blogs, podcasts, and conferences are just the tip of the iceberg. Webinars, YouTube channels, online forums, and social media groups also offer valuable avenues for learning and networking. Remember, diversity is key here - by casting your net wide, you can gain a more holistic view of the data science world.

Before we finish, here's an insider's tip: Start with a resource that resonates with you and aligns with your learning style. Do you prefer reading? Go for blogs. Is listening more your thing? Explore podcasts. Love meeting people and exchanging ideas? Look out for conferences. The resources you choose should fuel your enthusiasm, not make learning a chore.

emerging trends in data science

You've been sailing smoothly on the data science voyage so far, and now it's time to gaze into our crystal ball. Let's discuss what the future may hold for data science - what are the emerging trends that might shape our field in the coming years?

1. AutoML: Automation in Machine Learning

First on our list is AutoML (Automated Machine Learning). This concept revolves around automating the tedious parts of machine learning, such as feature engineering, model selection, hyperparameter tuning, and model validation. While a data scientist's intuition and expertise will always be invaluable, AutoML can save a tremendous amount of time and help avoid human errors. Tools such as Google's Cloud AutoML and DataRobot are making AutoML more accessible, and it's a trend worth watching.

2. Explainable AI (XAI)

As machine learning models become increasingly complex, they often become less interpretable. They're "black boxes," where it's unclear exactly how input data is transformed into output predictions. Enter

Explainable AI (XAI) - the movement towards creating AI models that are understandable and interpretable by humans. Given the growing demand for accountability and transparency in AI decisions, especially in sensitive areas like healthcare and finance, XAI is set to play a big role in future data science developments.

3. DataOps

DataOps is the application of DevOps principles to data analytics. It involves automated, agile, and collaborative techniques to improve the speed, quality, and usability of data analytics. Think continuous integration, automated testing, and rapid deployment - but for data. By enhancing the quality of data and ensuring its timely delivery to data scientists, DataOps can significantly streamline the data science process.

4. Edge Computing

Traditionally, data is sent from devices (like IoT devices) to a central location (like the cloud) for processing. But with edge computing, data processing occurs directly on the device, or "at the edge" of the network. This allows for quicker response times and less strain on network resources. As the Internet of Things (IoT) continues to grow, so does the demand for edge computing. Data scientists will need to adapt their techniques to accommodate this shift.

5. Privacy-preserving Machine Learning

In the age of GDPR and increasing concerns over

data privacy, protecting sensitive information is crucial. Privacy-preserving techniques such as differential privacy and federated learning are being explored to allow machine learning to be performed on encrypted data. This means models can be trained on a wealth of sensitive data without actually accessing the raw data itself, providing a groundbreaking way to gain insights while maintaining privacy.

6. Quantum Computing

Though still in its infancy, quantum computing holds enormous potential for data science. Quantum computers use the principles of quantum mechanics to process information in ways that traditional computers cannot match. They promise to solve complex optimization problems and perform certain types of machine learning much faster than existing computers. Though it may be a while before quantum computing becomes mainstream, it's a space to watch.

15 /
the future of data science

predicting data science trends

REMEMBER, data science is not just about crunching numbers; it's about understanding the past and using that understanding to predict the future. That's what we're doing here: we're going to put our data science hats on and think about how to foresee the trajectory of our very own field.

1. Staying Ahead of the Curve

When trying to predict trends, the first thing to remember is to stay aware. This means keeping an eye on relevant news, research, and discussions. Follow leading data science researchers and organizations on social media. Attend conferences and webinars. Read, read, and read some more. As the old saying goes, knowledge is power.

2. Understanding the Past

To predict the future, we must understand the past. Look at the trends that have defined data science so far. What were the hot topics five years ago? What about two years ago? Last year? How have these trends evolved? By understanding the trajectory of the field, you can make informed predictions about where it's heading.

3. Recognizing the Influencers

Influencers are individuals, organizations, or even events that have a significant impact on shaping trends. These could be tech giants like Google or Facebook, renowned researchers, or major incidents like data breaches or the introduction of new privacy laws. By recognizing and following these influencers, you can get a sense of the direction the field might take.

4. Following the Money

Follow the funding. Where is the investment money flowing? A significant influx of funding into a particular area of data science usually signals a trend on the rise. Keep an eye on venture capital funding, government grants, and research scholarships. Also, be aware of where big tech companies are investing their resources.

5. Being Aware of the Larger Tech Landscape

Data science doesn't exist in a vacuum. It's part of the larger tech ecosystem, and trends in data science are often linked to broader tech trends. Developments in areas such as AI, quantum computing, cloud computing, and cybersecurity can all have major implications for data science.

6. Utilizing Predictive Analytics Tools

There are many tools out there designed to help predict trends in various fields, including data science. These tools typically use machine learning algorithms to analyze large amounts of data and identify patterns and trends. Some popular ones include Google Trends and Exploding Topics. Use these tools, but use them wisely. Remember that they're just tools, and they're only as good as the person using them.

Predicting trends is not an exact science. It's part art, part science, and a whole lot of intuition and critical thinking. It requires staying informed, being observant, and constantly learning and adapting. But that's what makes it exciting, isn't it?

It's important to note that predicting trends isn't just about staying ahead of the game or having bragging rights. It's about understanding where our field is going so that we can make informed decisions about what skills to learn, what projects to undertake, and how to provide the most value in our jobs. It's about being proactive rather than reactive.

We're all a part of this vibrant, evolving field, and each of us has a role to play in shaping its future. In the next Section, we'll delve into another critical aspect of data science: ethical considerations. Remember, with great power comes great responsibility, and as data scientists, we wield a lot of power.

potential impact of data science in various sectors

Our journey together has already taken us far into the landscape of data science, and today, we're going to take a step back to look at the broader view. We're going to dive into the potential impact of data science across various sectors. As we do, let's remember that every industry has unique challenges and opportunities, and data science can play a unique role in each.

1. Healthcare: A Prescription for Improvement

In healthcare, data science can make a world of difference. From predicting disease outbreaks to personalized medicine, the possibilities are endless. Imagine using wearable devices to monitor vital signs in real time, enabling doctors to detect diseases like heart disease or diabetes at an early stage. Data science can also be used in managing healthcare resources, improving patient care, and even in the development of new drugs.

2. Agriculture: Cultivating a Better Future

It might be surprising, but agriculture is ripe for

data science innovation. Precision farming, which uses data to optimize farming practices, can increase yield and efficiency. Data science can help predict weather patterns and their impact on crops, monitor soil quality, and even help farmers make decisions about when to plant and harvest. It's not an overstatement to say data science could help us solve world hunger.

3. Finance: A Wealth of Opportunities

The finance industry has always been data-driven, but with the advent of data science, the possibilities have expanded exponentially. From predicting stock market trends to detecting fraudulent transactions, data science is revolutionizing the industry. Automated trading, personalized financial advice, and improved risk assessment are just a few of the applications.

4. Transportation: On the Road to Efficiency

Data science is driving major improvements in the transportation industry. Think about Uber's algorithm that matches drivers and riders or Waze's real-time traffic predictions. Predictive maintenance can help avoid equipment failures, while route optimization can save time and fuel. In the future, data science will play a crucial role in making self-driving cars a reality.

5. Education: Lessons in Innovation

Education is another sector where data science can make a big difference. Learning analytics can help teachers understand how students learn and tailor their teaching methods accordingly. It can also help identify students who might need extra help, predict future performance, and even design personalized learning paths.

6. Retail: A Personal Touch

The retail industry is another area where data science shines. Customer segmentation, personalized marketing, inventory management, and sales forecasting are all areas where data science is making an impact. For example, Amazon's recommendation engine, which suggests products based on past purchases, is a classic example of data science in action.

7. Government: Serving the Public Better

Last, but definitely not least, data science can greatly improve the way government serves the public. Predictive policing can help prevent crime, while data-driven policy decisions can lead to better outcomes. Data science can also improve transparency and help governments better understand the needs of their constituents.

These are just a few examples of how data science can impact different sectors. The possibilities are truly endless. Data science has the power to make our lives better in so many ways, and we're only just scratching the surface. That's what makes this field so exciting and rewarding to be a part of.

your role as a future data scientist

We're going to step away from the technologies, the methodologies, and the algorithms to focus on something far more personal – you. In particular, we're going to talk about your future role as a data scientist. What will you do? How will you make a difference? Let's dive in.

1. Truth Seeker: Unraveling the Mysteries of Data

First and foremost, as a data scientist, you will be a truth seeker. You'll dive deep into data, mining it for insights and using it to answer complex questions. You'll create models that illuminate patterns, and you'll use these insights to predict trends and influence strategies. Whether you're exploring customer behavior for a retail giant or analyzing health outcomes for a medical research institute, your primary role will be to extract truth and wisdom from data.

2. Problem Solver: Creating Innovative Solutions

Data science is all about problem-solving. You'll face business challenges that require creative, data-driven solutions. This might mean developing an algorithm to predict customer churn or creating a machine learning model to help diagnose disease. As a data scientist, you will have the opportunity to use your skills to tackle real-world problems and make a meaningful difference.

3. Storyteller: Bringing Data to Life

Another critical aspect of your role as a data scientist will be as a storyteller. While it's essential to dive deep into the data and extract insights, it's equally important to communicate these insights effectively to others. You'll be tasked with translating complex data findings into clear, compelling narratives that drive decision-making. You'll tell the story of the data in a way that everyone can understand.

4. Team Player: Collaborating for Success

Data science isn't a solo sport. You'll work closely with other professionals, like business analysts, engineers, and decision-makers, to turn data insights into actionable strategies. This means you'll need to be able to collaborate, communicate effectively, and understand the bigger business context. Being a team player is a critical part of being a successful data scientist.

5. Lifelong Learner: Staying Ahead of the Curve

Finally, as a data scientist, you'll need to be a lifelong learner. The field of data science is dynamic, with new technologies, methodologies, and best practices continually emerging. You'll need to stay curious, continuously updating your skills and knowledge to stay ahead of the curve. It's a challenge, but it's also one of the things that makes this field so exciting.

Now that we've explored the various roles you'll play as a future data scientist, it's important to remember that your journey is your own. There isn't a single "correct" way to be a data scientist. Your path will depend on your interests, your skills, and the opportunities that come your way.

Take the time to think about what kind of data scientist you want to be. What problems do you want to solve? What kind of impact do you want to have? Remember, as a data scientist, you have the potential to make a significant difference in the world. Use your powers wisely!

16 /
resources for
further learning

online courses and tutorials

IN THIS DIGITALLY-CONNECTED AGE, learning opportunities are no longer confined to physical classrooms or hefty textbooks. We live in a time where learning resources are just a click away, accessible to anyone, anytime, anywhere. As such, online courses and tutorials have become powerful tools in the arsenal of every aspiring data scientist. Ready to explore this vast landscape of digital knowledge? Let's dive in!

Online Courses

Online courses offer structured, comprehensive learning paths that mimic traditional classroom education, but with added flexibility. Here are some platforms and courses that are worth your attention:

1. Coursera

Coursera offers high-quality courses in partnership with top universities and institutions. For data science, courses like "Machine Learning" by Stanford University, and "Data Science" by Johns Hopkins University, are popular choices. These courses delve deep into the subjects and often come with interactive assignments to solidify your understanding.

2. edX

edX is another great platform offering university-level courses. It has a MicroMasters program in "Statistics and Data Science" from MIT, and a Professional Certificate in "Data Science" from Harvard University, which are renowned for their robust curriculum.

3. Udacity

Udacity offers what they call 'Nanodegrees' - compact, job-focused courses designed in collaboration with leading tech companies. The "Data Scientist" and "Data Analyst" nanodegrees are practical and industry-oriented, offering a mix of theory and hands-on projects.

Tutorials and Hands-On Learning

Learning by doing is arguably one of the most effective ways to master data science. Here are some platforms that offer practical tutorials and hands-on learning opportunities:

1. Kaggle

Kaggle is an invaluable resource for any aspiring data scientist. It offers a wealth of datasets to explore and experiment with, as well as competitions where you can test your skills. Additionally, Kaggle's "Learn" section provides micro-courses covering a range of data science topics, such as Python, Machine Learning, and Data Visualization.

2. DataCamp

DataCamp offers interactive courses focusing on data science and analytics. Their learning interface is unique as it allows you to write and run code right within the platform. Their courses cover a wide array of topics, from data manipulation with pandas to creating machine learning models with scikit-learn.

3. Project Euler

For those who love a good challenge, Project Euler offers a series of computational problems intended to be solved with computer programs. These problems can provide a fun way to improve your problem-solving and programming skills.

The world of online learning is incredibly vast, offering something for every learning style and skill level. Whether you prefer the structure of online courses or the practical focus of tutorials, there's a wealth of knowledge waiting for you. Start exploring, experimenting, and expanding your skillset. There's no limit to what you can learn!

data science communities and forums

You've made it this far, mastering concepts, working on projects, learning from books and online courses, but now we face a crucial piece of the puzzle: the human element. Welcome to the exciting world of data science communities and forums!

In data science, much like in other disciplines, you are not alone. You're part of a dynamic, supportive community of learners, professionals, and thought leaders, all passionate about data. Engaging with this community not only enhances your learning but also opens up opportunities for collaboration, networking, and mentorship. Let's explore some of these communities and forums that you can be a part of.

1. Stack Overflow

If you've ever searched for a coding problem online, chances are you've stumbled upon Stack Overflow. This platform is a massive Q&A forum where users can ask questions, provide answers, and engage in discussions on a wide range of programming topics. It's not uncommon to find threads with deep insights and nuanced explanations, so it's definitely worth diving into.

2. Kaggle

We mentioned Kaggle earlier in the context of its datasets and competitions, but it's worth noting that it's also a vibrant community. Kaggle forums are packed with discussions on different competitions, datasets, and general data science topics. They also have a feature called Kaggle Kernels (now called Kaggle Code), where users can share their code and analyses, making it a great place to learn from others' work.

3. GitHub

GitHub isn't a forum in the traditional sense, but it's an essential community platform for data scientists. You can follow repositories related to data science, contribute to open-source projects, or even create your own projects for others to collaborate on. GitHub is a brilliant place to learn from real-world projects and contribute to the field.

4. Reddit

Reddit hosts a number of communities (known as subreddits) dedicated to data science. Subreddits like r/datascience, r/machinelearning, and r/learnpython have active members who discuss industry trends, share resources, and provide answers to technical queries. Reddit's informal environment encourages spontaneous discussions and ideation.

5. LinkedIn and Twitter

Don't underestimate the power of professional and social networks! Following data scientists and organizations on LinkedIn and Twitter can keep you updated on the latest news, articles, and discussions in the field. You can engage in these discussions, share your own thoughts, and build a network in the process.

6. Meetup

Meetup.com can help you find local or virtual meetups on data science. These meetups can range from casual discussion groups to workshops and presentations. They're a fantastic way to learn new things, meet like-minded people, and sometimes even find mentors or job opportunities.

7. Data Science Central

Data Science Central is a niche online community with a focus on big data and analytics. They regularly host webinars and provide a forum for blogging and discussion, making it an excellent resource for both learning and networking.

Being part of these communities and forums can make your data science journey more engaging, enjoyable, and fruitful. The knowledge you gain from books and courses is enriched by discussions, problem-solving, and sharing within these platforms.

exercises

mini-project 1: data cleansing with python

PROMPT:

Find a publicly available dataset (for instance, from Kaggle or UCI Machine Learning Repository) and perform the following tasks:

- Load the data using pandas

    - Identify missing data and deal with them appropriately

    - Detect outliers and handle them

    - Do some basic exploratory data analysis (e.g., using pandas profiling)

. . .

Solution:

The solution will highly depend on the chosen dataset and the exact actions needed for that dataset, but here is a general approach in Python using pandas:

```python
import pandas as pd


# Load data
df = pd.read_csv('your_dataset.csv')


# Identify missing data
missing = df.isnull().sum()


# Handle missing data (remove or fill in with mean, median, or mode)
df = df.fillna(df.mean())


# Detect outliers (here, using the Z-score method)
from scipy.stats import zscore
z_scores = zscore(df)
abs_z_scores = abs(z_scores)
```

```
filtered_entries = (abs_z_scores < 3).all(axis=1)
df = df[filtered_entries]
```

```
# Basic EDA
import pandas_profiling
profile = pandas_profiling.ProfileReport(df)
profile.to_file("output.html")
```

mini-project 2: stock price predictor

Prompt:

Using a historical stock price dataset, build a simple predictive model using linear regression to predict future stock prices. You can use Python with libraries such as pandas for data manipulation and sklearn for building the predictive model.

Solution:

Below is a simple code snippet using Python. Remember, this is a very simple predictor and actual stock price prediction is a complex task involving many more factors.

. . .

```python
import pandas as pd
from sklearn.model_selection import train_test_split
from sklearn.linear_model import LinearRegression
from sklearn import metrics



# Load the dataset
df = pd.read_csv('stock_prices.csv')



# Choose 'date' as independent variable and 'close' as dependent variable
X = df['date'].values.reshape(-1,1)
y = df['close'].values.reshape(-1,1)



# Split the data into training and testing sets
X_train, X_test, y_train, y_test = train_test_split(X, y, test_size=0.2, random_state=0)



# Create the model and train it
regressor = LinearRegression()
regressor.fit(X_train, y_train)
```

· · ·

```
# Use the model to make predictions
    y_pred = regressor.predict(X_test)
    ```
```

Note: You'll need to preprocess the 'date' feature from a string to a numerical representation and possibly reshape your data before this step. Also, actual stock prediction is much more complex than this and takes several other features into consideration.

These are basic project solutions. Given the complexity and varying nature of data science projects, the actual implementation can vary a lot based on the specific problem, dataset, and chosen methodology.

## mini-project 3: sentiment analysis

Prompt:

Collect tweets about a trending topic and perform sentiment analysis on them. You can use Python's tweepy library to collect tweets and TextBlob to perform sentiment analysis.

Solution:
```

The detailed code will depend on the specifics, but a skeleton might look something like this:

```python
import tweepy
from textblob import TextBlob

# authentication keys (replace with your own)
consumer_key = 'YOUR-CONSUMER-KEY'
consumer_secret = 'YOUR-CONSUMER-SECRET'
access_token = 'YOUR-ACCESS-TOKEN'
access_token_secret = 'YOUR-ACCESS-TOKEN-SECRET'

auth = tweepy.OAuthHandler(consumer_key, consumer_secret)
auth.set_access_token(access_token, access_token_secret)
api = tweepy.API(auth)

public_tweets = api.search('Your Trending Topic')
```

. . .

```
for tweet in public_tweets:
    print(tweet.text)
    analysis = TextBlob(tweet.text)
    print(analysis.sentiment)
```

In this simple script, the sentiment property returns a namedtuple of the form Sentiment(polarity, subjectivity). The polarity score is a float within the range [-1.0, 1.0]. The subjectivity is a float within the range [0.0, 1.0] where 0.0 is very objective and 1.0 is very subjective.

mini-project 4: customer segmentation

Prompt:

Use a dataset of customer data for a hypothetical company and perform customer segmentation using clustering (KMeans, for instance). Your features might include frequency of purchase, average money spent, and time since last purchase.

Solution:

Here's a skeleton of what your Python code might look like:

```python
```

```
from sklearn.cluster import KMeans
import pandas as pd


# Load the data
data = pd.read_csv('customers.csv')


# select only the relevant features
data = data[['frequency', 'money_spent', 'time_s-
ince_last_purchase']]


# create a kmeans object
kmeans = KMeans(n_clusters=3)


# fit the data
kmeans.fit(data)


# get the cluster assignments for each data point
labels = kmeans.labels_
```

Remember to normalize or standardize your data before feeding it into the KMeans algorithm, as it's sensitive to the scale of the data.

. . .

The above projects are a starting point and can be expanded further depending upon individual requirements, datasets, and project goals. The solutions provided are basic Python code snippets showing the core task and can be extended further for error handling, data preprocessing, visualization and more.

mini-project 5: predicting housing prices

Prompt:

Using a dataset such as the Boston Housing dataset (which can be accessed through the sklearn library), build a model to predict housing prices based on various features. You can use linear regression, decision trees, or any other algorithm of your choice.

Solution:

A skeleton of Python code for this project might look like:

```python
from sklearn.datasets import load_boston
```

```
from sklearn.model_selection import train_test_split
from sklearn.linear_model import LinearRegression

# Load the dataset
boston = load_boston()

# Split the dataset
X_train, X_test, y_train, y_test = train_test_split(boston.data, boston.target, test_size=0.2, random_state=42)

# Build and train the model
lr = LinearRegression()
lr.fit(X_train, y_train)

# Test the model
predictions = lr.predict(X_test)
```

This is a simple implementation and doesn't include data exploration, feature selection, or model evaluation steps which you'd normally include in a data science project.

mini-project 6: news classification

Prompt:

Using a news dataset like the 20 Newsgroups dataset (available in sklearn), build a model to classify news into various topics.

Solution:

Here is a simplified version of Python code for this project:

```python
from sklearn.datasets import fetch_20newsgroups
from sklearn.feature_extraction.text import Tfidf-
Vectorizer
from sklearn.naive_bayes import MultinomialNB
from sklearn.pipeline import make_pipeline


# Load the dataset
data = fetch_20newsgroups()
                    . . .
```

```
# Split the dataset
    train_data = data.data[:10000]
    train_targets = data.target[:10000]
    test_data = data.data[10000:]
    test_targets = data.target[10000:]


# Create a pipeline: TF-IDF Vectorizer and Multinomial
Naive Bayes classifier
    model = make_pipeline(TfidfVectorizer(), Multin-
omialNB())


# Train the model
    model.fit(train_data, train_targets)


# Predict on new data
    predicted_categories = model.predict(test_data)
    ```
```

Remember that these are simplified projects, so you'll want to expand upon these ideas and include all necessary steps like data cleaning, exploration, feature engineering, model evaluation, etc. in a real-world project. Also, remember to handle exceptions and edge cases.
```

mini-project 7: sentiment analysis on social media

Prompt:

Perform sentiment analysis on a set of tweets about a recent trending topic. The challenge here is to extract tweets on a particular subject and then categorize the sentiment of the tweet. You can use Twitter APIs and a sentiment analysis library like TextBlob.

Solution:

An indicative Python code for this project:

```python
import tweepy
from textblob import TextBlob

# Authentication details. To obtain these, visit your
# Twitter Developer Account
consumer_key = 'CONSUMER_KEY_HERE'
consumer_secret = 'CONSUMER_SECRET_HERE'
access_token = 'ACCESS_TOKEN_HERE'
access_token_secret = 'ACCESS_TOKEN_SECRET_HERE'
```

. . .

```
# Create the API object
    auth    =    tweepy.OAuthHandler(consumer_key,
consumer_secret)
    auth.set_access_token(access_token,    access_to-
ken_secret)
    api = tweepy.API(auth)


# Collect tweets
    public_tweets = api.search('Your Trending Topic')


# Perform sentiment analysis
    for tweet in public_tweets:
    analysis = TextBlob(tweet.text)
    print(analysis.sentiment)
```

mini-project 8: image classification

Prompt:

Develop an image classification system using a Convolutional Neural Network (CNN). You can use the CIFAR-10 dataset, which consists of 60,000 32x32 color images in 10 classes.

. . .

Solution:

Here's a simple Python code for this project using Keras:

```python
from keras.datasets import cifar10
from keras.models import Sequential
from keras.layers import Dense, Flatten
from keras.layers.convolutional import Conv2D


# load dataset
(train_images, train_labels), (test_images, test_labels) = cifar10.load_data()


# normalize pixel values
train_images, test_images = train_images / 255.0, test_images / 255.0


# define the model
model = Sequential()
model.add(Conv2D(32, (3, 3), activation='relu',
```

```
input_shape=(32, 32, 3)))
    model.add(Flatten())
    model.add(Dense(64, activation='relu'))
    model.add(Dense(10))


# compile the model
    model.compile(optimizer='adam', loss=tf.keras.losses.SparseCategoricalCrossentropy(from_logits=True), metrics=['accuracy'])


# train the model
    model.fit(train_images, train_labels, epochs=10)


# evaluate the model
    test_loss, test_acc = model.evaluate(test_images, test_labels, verbose=2)
    ```
```

Please replace 'CONSUMER_KEY_HERE', 'CONSUMER_SECRET_HERE', 'ACCESS_TOKEN_HERE', and 'ACCESS_TOKEN_SECRET_HERE' with your actual Twitter API credentials.

. . .
```

Remember to handle exceptions, edge cases, and follow all necessary steps like data cleaning, exploration, feature engineering, model evaluation, etc., in a real-world project.

mini-project 9: real-time face recognition

Prompt:

Create a real-time face recognition system using OpenCV and Dlib libraries. Your application should be able to recognize faces from your webcam feed in real-time.

Solution:

Here's a simple Python code for this project:

```python
import cv2
import dlib
from skimage import io

# Initialize dlib's face detector
detector = dlib.get_frontal_face_detector()
```

. . .

```
# Initialize function to create a bounding box around
the detected faces
    def draw_rectangle(image, bounds):
    x, y, w, h = bounds
    cv2.rectangle(image, (x, y), (x + w, y + h), (0, 255,
0), 2)



# Start capturing the WebCam
    video_capture = cv2.VideoCapture(0)



while True:
    ret, frame = video_capture.read()
    gray    =    cv2.cvtColor(frame,    cv2.COLOR_B-
GR2GRAY)



# Detect faces in the grayscale image
    faces = detector(gray)



# Draw a rectangle around the faces
        for rect in faces:
        draw_rectangle(frame,    (rect.left(),    rect.top(),
```

```
rect.width(), rect.height()))


# Display the resulting image
    cv2.imshow('Video', frame)


# Break the loop if 'q' key is pressed
    if cv2.waitKey(1) & 0xFF == ord('q'):
        break


video_capture.release()
    cv2.destroyAllWindows()
    ```
```

# mini-project 10: text-to-speech (tts) application

Prompt:

Create a Text-to-Speech application where you input a sentence and the system generates an audio file with that speech using Google Text-to-Speech (gTTS).

Solution:

Here's a Python code for this project:
```

. . .

```python
from gtts import gTTS
import os


# Define your text
my_text = "Hello, welcome to data science world!"


# Language in which you want to convert
language = 'en'



# Create gTTS object
my_obj = gTTS(text=my_text, lang=language, slow=False)


# Save the speech audio into a file
my_obj.save("welcome.mp3")


# Play the audio file
os.system("welcome.mp3")
```

. . .

Please remember, for any real-world project, it's important to consider performance, error handling, and code organization. These examples provide a basic understanding of the process. Depending on the complexity of your project, you might need to add more steps.